Out of the Shadows: Revealing the Path to Recovery

By
Mark Litzsinger with Sarah Hamaker

Out of the Shadows: Revealing the Path to Discovery
By Mark Litzsinger
with Sarah Hamaker

ISBN: Perfect Bound 978-0-9980204-0-24
ePub 978-0-9980204-1-9
ePDF 978-0-9980204-2-6
LCCN: 2017957799

Printed in the United States of America

To Bonnie Senner, Dr. Bill Scheftner, Dick and Dona Litzsinger, and my siblings, Robin, Heidi, Shawn, and Todd. Without your encouragement, support, listening skills, patience, and medical knowledge, I would probably not be here today and would not have been able to write this book with the help of the lovely Sarah Hamaker and her wonderful support staff, including Connor Stratman and researcher Whitney Hopler.

No one goes through life for free. There are many bumps on the road through life. We all face challenges, regardless of our economic standing. Dedication and perseverance are the keys to overcoming these obstacles, and each hurdle conquered makes us stronger and better capable of handling the next bump.

Table of Contents

Foreword

Wʜᴀᴛ'ѕ ʜᴀᴘᴘᴇɴɪɴɢ ᴛᴏ ᴛʜᴇ ᴍᴇɴᴛᴀʟ ʜᴇᴀʟᴛʜ ᴏꜰ Aᴍᴇʀɪᴄᴀɴѕ ᴍᴀʏ surprise and shock you. In any given year, 43.8 million adults experience mental illness. By diagnosis, approximately 1 percent of the population lives with schizophrenia, 2.6 percent with bipolar disorder, 6.9 percent with major depression (Mark's disease), and 18 percent with anxiety disorders. One in five children between the ages of 13 and 18 has, or will have, a serious mental illness. Suicide is the second leading cause of death in youth between the ages of 15 and 24, and 90 percent of those had an underlying mental illness.

With this startling prevalence in our society, you might ask why isn't there more dialogue to gain understanding and to ensure adequate treatment and support for families and persons living with a mental illness. The problem is simple: Mental illness is still seen as a stigma. The stigma is rooted in our history when it was an embarrassment for families to have a member with mental illness. Many considered a mental illness or addiction a moral failure instead of an illness. It is time we move beyond these out-of-date conceptions and get educated.

Stigma keeps the conversation down. It isolates the person with a mental illness and usually that person's family too. It prevents others from understanding and helping. Stories are an excellent way to reduce stigma. Intellectual descriptions of mental illness help somewhat, but stories are the best vehicle for learning, especially when the stories are from someone you know. For then it becomes clear that although mental illness is a disease of the brain, there is a real person there too, who may function quite well at times.

Mark's very personal story about his own battle with depression helps us understand why we need books like this. He describes his brothers, sisters, and others worrying about his erratic behavior. His parents struggled with understanding what was going on during his periods of severe depression. As chairman of a billion-dollar company, he had nowhere to hide.

When I read the first edition of this book, there were times I almost asked aloud, "Where were those who could educate the family on the disease?" A person's support system, family, friends, and work colleagues can't help if they don't know what is going on. For Mark, how scary this period must have been, wondering what was happening to him and why couldn't he live up to his expectations for himself. Through sharing like Mark has done in this book, others can become aware of the disease, symptoms, treatments, and the need for support for both the person living with a mental illness, and those caring for that person.

I have my own personal journey, once having been one of two helpless parents trying to do our best for a child with mental illness. That led both my wife and I to the National Alliance on Mental Illness (NAMI), a national organization with state and local chapters dedicated to education, advocacy, and support for families and persons living with a mental illness. A signature program of NAMI is "Family to Family," a 12-week class taught by peers for caregivers, designed to enable them to take the leadership with their loved one in understanding the disease, ensuring support mechanisms are in place, and advocating for their care. What a shame this program did not come to the attention of Mark's family.

We need to get more comfortable in talking about mental illness, its symptoms, treatments, and needed support. Sensational news accounts of bizarre or dangerous behavior of someone with a mental illness need to be balanced by stories of people struggling with the disease, but still trying to be productive persons in our world. Mark accomplished this in writing his book.

We need to educate our legislators so they realize mental illness is just another illness, one of the brain. Medical care needs to be available to those with mental illness, something that for too long had only limited coverage in health insurance policies. As a result of insurance restrictions, and lack of government programs, currently the support network for mental illness is weak. Mark had the benefit of being able to afford the best in treatment, but not everyone is so lucky.

But there is hope. The National Institute of Mental Health is funding research in new exciting directions. The ability to see results through brain scans helps accelerate understanding. Data-driven research is opening many new avenues. We hope that we can move beyond treating symptoms to finding some cures. But we should not minimize the importance of treating symptoms to help the person with the disease improve to the point where he or she can lead a more normal life. There is now a much more active dialogue on mental illness, and that can lead to more understanding and support.

John Schladweiler
Board President
NAMI Illinois
August 2017

Introduction

"But with the slow menace of a glacier, depression came on. No one had any measure of its progress; no one had any plan for stopping it. Everyone tried to get out of its way."
—Frances Perkins, U.S. Secretary of Labor from 1933 to 1945

IMAGINE A FOG THAT PERMEATES EVERY ASPECT OF YOUR LIFE. IT clouds your thinking. It muddles your brain. It makes it difficult to refocus your attention. It's like you're living as a ghost, watching the real world from afar. That's how some have described what living with depression feels like.

Others talk about depression as a dark place, falling into a bottomless shaft, drowning, and having no joy. Sometimes depression is described as nothingness, torture, or a cancer of the soul. Still others say depression makes them feel like they're in a whirlpool, a constant circle with no exit.

That's an apt description for how I felt when depressed. For me, depression was a continuous circle, an ever-deepening gulf that sucked me down for months at a time. All I ever wanted was to be a normal person with a normal job. Then depression hit me again and again and again, taking years of my life.

My story isn't unique—those who suffer from depression will recognize glimpses of themselves in my trajectory. But by sharing my experience, I hope to encourage others to seek help. I also hope to provide guidance for families and friends fighting alongside those with depression, helping them to get to a healthier place. This is my story, but it's also everyone's story who suffers from depression.

I first encountered depression as I was about to embark on the first part of my adult life after college. Up to that point in my life, I had had many successes, including playing on two state championship tennis teams at Hinsdale Central High School in Hinsdale, Illinois. I had many friends—and girlfriends—throughout high school and college, and was the president of the Phi Kappa Sigma fraternity while at Texas Christian University in Fort Worth, Texas.

As the oldest of five and the eldest grandchild, I was expected to set a good example for my siblings and cousins. For the most part, I lived up to my family's expectations—that doesn't mean my friends and I didn't occasionally party on the weekends and drink, which we did, but overall I stayed on the straight and narrow.

When I went off to Texas Christian University in 1974, I played tennis for the university and joined Phi Kappa Sigma. I went to class, got good grades, played tennis, and partied with my frat brothers, but still managed to graduate in four years.

After graduation, I wasn't sure what career I wanted to pursue, so when there was a chance to work at my family's company, the Follett Corporation, I took it. I started my career there in the College Bookstore Division (Follett College Stores). The 145-year-old company, headquartered in Westchester, Illinois, is a lease operator of college bookstores—among other businesses—in the educational marketplace. The Follett Corporation is a 3.6 billion-dollar company started in 1873, before being taken over by my great-grandfather C.W. Follett, in the early years of the twentieth century.

My first position in the college bookstore division was as a management trainee at the bookstore at Saddleback Community College in Mission Viejo, California. I was lucky enough to choose where I would do my training. Of course, I wanted to go to California because of the good-looking women in their bikinis, the music, and the laid-back lifestyle—you can tell my priorities in starting a new job were way off. I was able to afford a nice apartment and a car on a starting salary of 8 thousand dollars per year.

I had been in California for approximately three months when one morning I woke up in my bed and stared at the ceiling instead of getting up right away. I knew something was wrong. I felt down and lonely. I signed up for a class at the college so that I could see the college psychologist to see what was going on. After a few sessions—including one in which he tried to hypnotize me—I could tell that seeing this particular doctor wasn't working.

The only relative living near me in California was my grandmother, who resided in West Lake Village. I visited her and told her how I was feeling. She was comforting and supportive, but despite her efforts, I continued on a downward spiral. Finally, after six months, I talked to the regional manager of the bookstore division about transferring back to the Illinois area to be closer to home, thinking that I might just be homesick. He transferred me to the off-campus bookstore at the University of Illinois in Champaign, Illinois.

I became one of the assistant managers of the store while still in training. Within a two- to three-month period, my depression seemed to go away. I now know this is called "cycling out." I was happy again and learned a lot at the store over the next two years. Then things began to unravel again, and this time it wasn't an easy climb back to "normal."

Many people don't know they have depression after their first episode. Like me, you might think that you just aren't feeling well. Perhaps you hope these emotions will pass and you'll get back to the status quo on your own. That didn't happen for me after the first initial episode. When I experienced other bouts with depression, I needed professional help to recover. The assistance of several doctors and therapists, working alongside me, provided the means to push me on the road to recovery.

What I'm trying to do within these pages is offer patients, potential patients, families, friends, and doctors encouragement and education about depression. This is a disease that doctors still don't completely understand. This is a disease that some who suffer from it still don't want to talk about it with their families or doctors. This is a disease that doesn't always completely go away. This is a disease that can take years to come to a place of wellness.

"The public's view of depression is really influenced by several things," says Dr. William Scheftner, psychopharmacologist and former chairman of the Department of Psychiatry at Rush University Medical Center in Chicago, Illinois.[1] "First, depression tends to be a recurrent and sometimes chronic illness. No matter how well intentioned one is, if you're living with someone who every two years feels awful and can't function to pull his share of the load, it becomes difficult to be accepting of this as an illness.

"Second, there's been a terrible misuse of the word *bipolar* by the media. Every ax-murderer or kid who goes berserk and shoots his parents is labeled as having a bipolar disorder," continues Dr. Scheftner. "And the vast majority don't clinically appear to be bipolar at all but have some illness like schizophrenia or other mental illness. Sometimes, I think the public's perception of depression is directly related to the latest tragic event."

Wherever you are on this journey—whether you're the patient, a family member, part of the medical profession, or ancillary services—increasing your knowledge and understanding of how depression impacts patients and family members, how the past has shaped current treatment methods, and what the future holds for those who suffer from this disease will provide a firm foundation from which to go forward. The goal of this book is to do just that—to give patients, family members, doctors, and others who wish to learn more a blueprint of the disease's history and treatments, as well as offer hope for a future in recovery.

Part I
The Disease

Chapter 1

A Brief History of Depression

"That's the thing about depression: A human being can survive almost anything, as long as she sees the end in sight. But depression is so insidious, and it compounds daily, that it's impossible to ever see the end. The fog is like a cage without a key."
—Elizabeth Wurtzel, American author of *Prozac Nation*

LIKE MOST DISEASES OF THE MIND, DEPRESSION HAS BEEN misunderstood, mislabeled, and misdiagnosed throughout the ages. Before we can delve into what we know about depression today, we need to take a brief look back at how depression has been viewed and treated in the past.

Although people have suffered from depression throughout recorded history, our opinion of the disease has changed dramatically over the years. We've come a long way in our understanding about what may cause depression and how best to treat it. "The story of depression is one in which we seem to witness a comparatively consistent disease phenomenon that is nevertheless endlessly [re-conceptualized] and lived according to the experience of the particular culture and individual concerned."[2]

From the ancient world's "melancholia" to the Enlightenment's more natural view of depression on to the twentieth century's more scientific viewpoint, depression has evolved from a state of mind to a disease with genetic traits. Let's examine the changes throughout the years in how the medical profession handled depression.

MELANCHOLIA

Documented reports of people afflicted by this disease go back to ancient Mesopotamia. Texts from this early human civilization describe people suffering from symptoms that match what we currently call depression, but which has been called different names—one being "melancholia"—in different time periods.

From the first reports about the disease when human writing first developed (between 1,000 and 2,000 B.C.) until the end of the Middle Ages in the 1400s A.D., the predominant view on depression was that it was caused by evil spirits (demons) who were possessing the souls of depressed people. However, Hippocrates, the ancient Greek physician, dissented from this view with his belief that all illnesses were caused by imbalanced bodily fluids. According to Hippocrates, depression resulted from people having too much black bile in their spleens.

Treatments for depression from ancient times through the Middle Ages varied widely. The treatments—designed to banish evil spirits and to prevent evil from spreading and infecting others—included

- exorcism,
- torture,
- burning, and
- drowning.

In ancient times, people suffering from depression often felt religious guilt because of their illness, fearing that their own sin was to blame for causing the disease and that if they could only try hard enough to avoid sin, they would get better. They felt shame, as well, when other believers assumed that God was punishing them through their disease.

Those in agreement with Hippocrates' belief that depression had a physical cause suggested less-extreme treatments for the disease, such as

- bloodletting,
- diet changes,
- herbal remedies,
- exercise, and
- bathing.

A MORE ENLIGHTENED VIEW

During the Renaissance, from the fourteenth to the seventeenth century, the predominant view on depression was that the disease was caused by natural (rather than supernatural) factors. The previous emphasis on spiritual warfare changed to a focus on physical and mental issues. Depressed people were advised to consider how the state of their bodies and minds might be causing their depression. Physical treatments like the ones Hippocrates had suggested became more popular.

People of the Renaissance era also began to consider mental treatments after the publication in 1621 of the landmark book *The Anatomy of Melancholy* by Robert Burton, which argued that causes for depression went beyond spiritual and physical health, and could include poverty and loneliness. Burton suggested treating depressed patients via means such as friendship, marriage, travel, and listening, which were designed to improve the overall quality of their lives.

In the Age of Enlightenment (1700s and early 1800s), many people thought that depression was caused by an inherent weakness in a person's temperament. Although depression was still treated, the purpose of treatment was no longer to cure the disease—because a cure wasn't thought to be possible—but to lessen the severity of it. This predominant view led to many depressed people being shunned as hopeless cases by society and ending up homeless or locked away in mental institutions.

The late 1800s saw the development of modern psychiatry, which revolutionized the way people thought about depression. Early, influential psychiatrists like Sigmund Freud theorized that depression was a result of people suffering significant losses in their lives. These doctors or psychiatrists pointed to both mental and physical factors as contributors to depression, noting that evidence of the disease could be found in depressed people's brains. In 1895, Emil Kraepelin, a German psychiatrist, officially classified depression as a disease in the new medical field of psychiatry.

"As ways of understanding the human mind and body were profoundly transformed within a modern scientific framework, 'the emotions' as an all-compassing category and process that was at once physiological and psychological—and not necessarily subject to volition—soon eclipsed its spiritual predecessors in medico-scientific literature."[3]

The current concept of depression gained ground during the late nineteenth century and "continues to evolve in the present day."[4] Once again, people began to believe that there was hope those suffering from depression could be cured. But many treatments for the disease from the late 1800s until the mid-1900s were daunting. Treatments included

- psychiatric counseling,
- electroshock,
- water immersion, and
- lobotomy (surgically severing connections in the brain's prefrontal lobes).

A TWENTIETH-CENTURY OBSERVATION

During the 1950s, a view emerged that there were two basic types of depression and that they should be treated differently according to their different causes. Endogenous depression originated within the brain, whereas neurotic depression came from factors in depressed people's environments.

The discovery, in 1952, that a medication called isoniazid used to treat tuberculosis also was effective at treating depression led many doctors to begin prescribing medications to treat depression. "In post–World War II United States, a lot of people had TB, and it turned out that one of the anti-tubercular agents—something called MAOIs [monoamine oxidase inhibitors]—actually worked as an antidepressant as well," explains Dr. Scheftner. "As these antidepressants were developed, people began to see a connection between medication helping depressed people, which meant there had to be something physiologic or physically involved in depression."

Thus, although people suffering from depression still pursued psychiatric therapy like counseling, many also began to take medicine for their condition. A new class of drugs called "antidepressants" debuted in 1957.

"The first antidepressant to gain widespread use was imipramine, the first drug in the tricyclic antidepressant family," says Dr. Scheftner. (See Chapter 9 for more on depression treatments of the twentieth century.) "Antidepressants have resulted in moral, political, and social debates over depression. ... Yet depression goes far beyond medication. Considered by psychiatric epidemiology as the most common mental disorder since 1970, it has a vaster and more complex history than simply as an emblem of psychopharmacology. And it is at the heart of the tensions of modern individualism. This is why we need to listen less to the antidepressant and more to the spirit of depression."[5]

THE MAINSTREAMING OF DEPRESSION

The arrival of Prozac in 1988 helped to "normalize" depression. That drug—the most widely prescribed antidepressant medication so far in history—has been touted by many in the medical profession as a simple solution for depression that tends to cause fewer side effects than other antidepressants while elevating patients' moods. The prevalence of people taking Prozac for a host of reasons, including depression, helped to remove some of the stigma of mental illness. (See Chapter 2 for more on how depression was, and is, perceived by society.)

The current views on treating depression take into account a wide array of possible contributing factors. Patients and their doctors can now choose from a host of physical, mental, emotional, and spiritual treatments to try to improve their quality of life while managing depression. These treatments include medications, psychiatric counseling, exercise, diet and sleep changes, stress reduction, and prayer.

Medical professionals are still learning what may cause depression, as well as how best to treat the disease. Depression has "ended up being the label that includes all of modern humanity's suffering. ... Depression speaks to us of illness, unhappiness, misfortune, and failure. ... We have trouble seeing clearly because depression, far from being a problem of distinguishing the normal from the pathological, brings together such a diversity of symptoms that the difficulty of defining and diagnosing it is a constant fact of psychiatry."[6]

Even as depressed people and those who seek to help them grapple with determining causes and treatments, more and more people are diagnosed with the disease. "According to The Royal College of Psychiatrists [in the United Kingdom], 'by 2020 it is estimated that depression will be the second most common disabling condition in the world,' a figure it derives from the World

Health Organization. Depression is, it seems, rapidly becoming a global threat."[7]

Many times those who have depression don't even realize they're sick. I had no idea I had it when I experienced my first bout with depression as a young college graduate. I just knew I felt like crap—not necessarily from a physical standpoint but from a mental standpoint. For me, it was like losing a baseball game and having a continuous feeling of being down.

What many people don't realize is that depression may have a genetic link. "The family studies coming out indicate that people who have depression are much more likely to have family histories of depressions," notes Dr. Scheftner. "That is to say they are more likely to have a first-degree relative—a mother, father, brother, or sister—who also suffer from depression."

My own experience, which is by no means unusual, underscores the importance of depression screening. In January 2016, the U.S. Preventive Services Task Force recommended that "all American adults should be screened for depression as part of their normal health-care routine."[8] This move recognizes how common depression has become, with researchers finding an increase in the mental illness recently related to the stress and fears of modern life.

Although only a doctor can provide an accurate diagnosis, here are the eleven most common symptoms of depression, according to Bethesda, Maryland's National Institute of Mental Health:

1. Difficulty concentrating, remembering details and making decisions;
2. Fatigue and decreased energy;
3. Feelings of guilt, worthlessness, and/or helplessness;
4. Feelings of hopelessness and/or pessimism;
5. Insomnia, early-morning wakefulness, or excessive sleeping;

6. Irritability, restlessness;

7. Loss of interest in activities or hobbies once pleasurable, including sex;

8. Overeating or appetite loss;

9. Persistent aches or pains, headaches, cramps, or digestive problems that do not ease even with treatment;

10. Persistent sad, anxious, or "empty" feelings; and

11. Thoughts of suicide, suicide attempts.

If you have experienced several of these symptoms over an extended period of time, please see your primary-care physician for a depression screening. If you suspect a family member may be depressed, strongly urge the person to see a doctor immediately. What we now know about depression is that with the assistance of doctors, medications, and therapy, people with depression can recover and have happy, fulfilled lives.

Behavioral Health Screen

This is an example of the type of screening mental health professionals will give to patients with depressive symptoms. Note that this is not for diagnostic purposes but for informational purposes. Please consult your own medical professionals for screening for depression.

During the last two weeks, how often have you been bothered by the following problems (check one in each row):

	Some days	More than half the days	Nearly every day
1. Little interest in doing things.			
2. Feeling down, depressed, or hopeless.			
3. Poor appetite or overeating.			

4. Feeling bad about yourself, that you're a failure, or that you've let your family down.			
5. Thoughts that you would be better off dead or of hurting yourself.			
6. Moving or speaking so slowly others have noticed. Or being too fidgety or restless to sit still and others have noticed.			
7. Trouble falling asleep or sleeping too much.			
8. Feeling very tired or having little energy.			
9. Trouble concentrating on reading, watching a show, etc.			
10. Feeling nervous or anxious or on edge; worrying about a lot of different things.			
11. Inability to control worrying. Ruminating on the same things over and over.			
12. Muscle tension, aches, or soreness.			
13. Becoming easily annoyed or irritable.			

Rate your level of function in the following areas:
0 to 10, ranging from not at all to mildly to moderately to markedly to extremely
Have the above symptoms disrupted your work or school life?
Have the above symptoms disrupted your social life?
Have the above symptoms disrupted your family or home responsibilities?

Chapter 2

Depression's Stigma

"I think this man might be useful to me—if my black dog returns. He seems quite away from me now—it is such a relief. All the [colors] come back into the picture."
—Winston Churchill, prime minister of the United Kingdom (1940 to 1945, 1951 to 1955), in a letter to his wife

NOT ONLY DO DEPRESSED PEOPLE SUFFER FROM THE HEALTH effects of the disease, they also often suffer from the stigma of having depression in American society. Cultural stereotypes about depression, which are often reinforced by mainstream media, still fuel negative attitudes toward people with the condition. The stigma of depression as a personal weakness rather than a legitimate medical condition persists despite efforts by those who treat depressed patients to educate the public. However, the stigma seems to be lessening as people who live with the condition—including public figures and celebrities—speak up about their own experiences with depression.

Because of the complex nature of depression, the stigmatization of those with the disease has led to discrimination and other injustices. Depression affects the personal identity and social communication of the person suffering from it, which in turn can create difficulties in getting help, contribute to social isolation, and lead to distress. "It can lead to feelings of guilt, anger, and anxiety, and is a pervasive phenomenon. Stigma can come from family members, from work colleagues, from health-care professionals, educators, and members of the general community."[9]

In general, stigma envelopes the negative response of society toward a perceived flaw in someone's personal character. That perception usually leads to discrimination and prejudice against the individual. The stigma related to depression has been lessening of late, but it's still quite common for those with depression to experience bias and judgment.[10]

A RESULT OF PERSONAL WEAKNESS

The main assumption that contributes to the stigma of depression is that the disease is somehow a character flaw, a personal weakness in those who suffer from it. This attitude can result in the mistreatment of people with depression. "Two thousand years of humiliation, mistrust, out-casting, punishment, and general antipathy will leave its effect on how we currently feel about people with depression."[11]

Because of this historical stigma, people suffering from depression are not encouraged to "put their hands up and identify themselves with a history of supposed malingerers, sinners, sexual miscreants, and lazy and self-obsessed serial complainers, who drain the personal and financial resources of others."[12] Depression has become linked to a sense that those with depression could be threatening or objectionable to interact with, as well as somehow liable for having the disease in the first place.[13]

During my last major depressive episode, which happened when I was chairman of my family's company, I struggled but held it together for the most part. But I was a little paranoid about how people were viewing me, asking myself: "Do they see any symptoms?" Of course, this is something you're not sharing with anybody. You end up walking around thinking that people might be picking up on the fact that you're acting a little different. And you also wonder how people would react if they knew the truth—that you are someone who suffers from depression.

But that mindset is slowly changing. DestinyBlue, a London-based artist who suffers from depression, uses her art to show what the disease feels like. Her emotionally charged, colorful, and imaginative art conveys depression in a vivid form. "I didn't come from an expressive household, and here I was with so much inside me—so much I didn't understand, thoughts, feelings, and emotions marched through me like an invading army," DestinyBlue told HuffPost in an August 2017 interview.[14] "I needed a way to process and vent, and drawing provided a canvas to untangle myself upon."

As DestinyBlue shares how crippling depression can be to its sufferers through her words and art, she's helping to unravel the mysteriousness of mental illness and giving people a glimpse of a better tomorrow. "I want others who are also struggling with mental health issues to know there is hope, and that they are not alone, and that someone else understands how tough a path it is to walk, and how strong you are for carrying on," she said in the HuffPost interview.

A RESULT OF PERSONAL CHOICES

Society's stigma against depression as a personal weakness also implies that somehow the people who suffer from depression made decisions that led to their depression, which means they must be personally at fault for being depressed. Even though medical knowledge has now progressed to the point where it's clear that biological changes to people's brains play key roles in depression, public perception often characterizes people with depression as somehow being to blame for their condition.

Since the turn of the twenty-first century, scientific evidence has emerged that shows depression's roots "in a malfunctioning brain, not unlike many other neurological disorders. But although brain disorders such as Alzheimer's disease, Parkinson's disease, and stroke may be viewed with compassion, a mental illness such as depression is too often seen as a sign of personal weakness."[15] (See Chapter 10 for more on treatments and understanding of depression in the twenty-first century.)

Efforts by family, friends, and employers to "try to shake the sufferer out of their depressive stupor ... are usually about as effective as telling a heart attack or stroke victim to 'run it off.'"[16] These comments are singularly unhelpful because depression is not a life choice. Depressed people can't simply *choose* not to be depressed.

Anyone can develop depression, regardless of their personal choices in life. "The history of our family shows we are the poster family for depression," says my sister Shawn Stratman.[17] "That's why when we talk about it, we're just so sad because it's an evil disease. It takes your joy. I hope it's less misunderstood now."

DEPRESSION PORTRAYALS

It's no secret that the way the mainstream media, including television shows, movies, and the Internet, portrays different groups of people influences how many Americans think about people in those groups. Unfortunately for people with depression, the media has often portrayed them in negative ways that perpetuate the stigma of depression as a personal weakness.

For example, television news programs and newspaper articles often stress a history of mental illness when describing a violent criminal's background. In addition, comedians use those with mental illness as fodder for jokes, while pharmaceutical company advertisements often exaggerate mental illness images to push their products.[18]

Movies also play influential roles in shaping how Americans think about depression. "Hollywood films can perpetuate curious beliefs regarding the mental illness spectrum. ... The victims of mental illness are often portrayed as aggressive, unpredictable, and dangerous, with psychiatrists commonly essayed as inept or manipulative."[19]

When the media does portray depressed people in positive ways as normal people, it can help lessen negative stereotypes. "Ironically, the media are also powerful partners for eradicating stigma. Education is the antidote to inaccurate beliefs and unfair behavior. By presenting depression as just another illness—and a very common and treatable one at that—the media can have a major impact on public opinion."[20]

One famous person from the twentieth century who struggled with depression is Winston Churchill. Born into a politically prominent family, Churchill suffered from depression all his life. His father, Lord Randolph Churchill, the eighth Duke of Marlborough, had psychotic episodes, and his daughter Diana eventually committed suicide after having had major depressive episodes throughout her life.[21]

Some scholars credit Churchill's experience with depression— which he called his "black dog"—as the force behind his drive to equip England against the growing threat of fascism in Germany prior to World War II. As psychiatrist and historian Anthony Storr points out, "Only a man who knew what it was to discern a gleam of hope in a hopeless situation, whose courage was beyond reason and whose aggressive spirit burned at its fiercest when he was hemmed in and surrounded by enemies, could have given emotional reality to the words of defiance which rallied and sustained us in the menacing summer of 1940."[22] (See "Depression Can Affect Anyone" on page 20 for a partial list of famous people with depression.)

DISCOURAGING TREATMENT

Unfortunately, depressed people who are embarrassed or ashamed about their mental health condition sometimes choose not to seek treatment. If depressed people do start treatment but then feel stigmatized for doing so, they may discontinue treatment.

For my father's generation and older generations, the image of insane asylums (especially as depicted in the movie *One Flew Over the Cuckoo's Nest*) as awful places where crazy people were locked up is still vivid. "Those memories put depression in a category you don't talk about," says my father, Dick Litzsinger.[23] "It was something you hid in public. That's the reason, over time, that these seminars Mark does at Rush University Medical Center in Chicago, Illinois, and books like this will go a long way to dispelling that silence. These measures will get people able to talk about it."

A celebrity feud between actor Tom Cruise and actress Brooke Shields in 2005 drew the public's attention to the ongoing misconceptions about depression. Cruise criticized Shields during a television interview with Matt Lauer on the NBC show *Today* for taking an antidepressant medication for her postpartum depression, asserting that she shouldn't need to rely on a drug to treat depression. Cruise basically said that there is no such thing as a chemical imbalance and that Shields could simply exercise and eat a nutritious diet to make her depression go away.

Shields responded in an op-ed piece for the *New York Times* called "War of Words." In the article, Shields writes that she felt "compelled to speak not just for myself but also for the hundreds of thousands of women who have suffered from postpartum depression."[24] Adding that, "to suggest that I was wrong to take drugs to deal with my depression, and that instead I should have taken vitamins and exercised shows an utter lack of understanding about postpartum depression and childbirth in general. If any good can come of Mr. Cruise's ridiculous rant, let's hope that it gives much-needed attention to a serious disease."[25]

In the workplace, companies are also beginning to destigmatize mental illness by drafting policies that encourage employees to take time off work to address issues like depression and anxiety. A *Wall Street Journal* article touted several such companies, like Ernst & Young, American Express Co., and Prudential Financial, which offered employee assistance programs, on-site access to mental health professionals, and free counseling.[26]

A FRESH VIEW

When public figures take the risk of damaging their reputations by admitting that they're struggling with depression in their own lives, many Americans take notice, and discussions about depression and its stigma move to the forefront of our cultural dialogue for a time.

Shields, who also chronicled her battle with depression in *Down Came the Rain: My Journey Through Postpartum Depression*, wrote that as a celebrity, she was making an intentional effort to try to decrease society's stigma of people who suffer from depression. In the op-ed article, Shields notes she had heard from many other depressed people who felt stigmatized, stating: "Since writing about my experiences with the disease, I have been approached by many women who have told me their stories and thanked me for opening up about a topic that is often not discussed because of fear, shame, or lack of support and information. Experts estimate that one in ten women suffer, usually in silence, with this treatable disease."[27]

The most powerful public reaction to the stigma of depression in recent years came about after the death of actor Robin

Williams in 2014. Although Williams had been depressed for many years, he hadn't spoken much publicly about his struggle with the disease. His suicide caused widespread shock and prompted discussion about depression in both mainstream and social media.

The reaction may have been especially powerfully in Williams' case because of the sharp dichotomy between his public face and private one. Publicly, Williams was known for making people laugh with his brilliant and outlandish comedy. Privately, Williams struggled with depression and substance abuse. In addition, an autopsy revealed that he suffered from Lewy body dementia, which causes hallucinations and disorientation.[28]

The shock of his death by suicide provided a needed wake-up call to everyone that mental illness is an oppressive force. "As the public registered the finality of his absence, social media became an outlet not only for heartfelt remembrances, but also messages of hope and compassion. This widespread empathy, matched by private conversations around the dinner table and water cooler, is a new phenomenon that demonstrates just how much the stigma of suicide has diminished in recent years."[29]

Author J.C. Arkham was among those who shared personal experiences with depression after Williams' death. In his book *Claims Department: Robin Williams Memorial: Comedian, Actor, Legend*, Arkham writes: "This man's sense of humor got me through all the tough times growing up. It was like losing an uncle I dearly loved. There's nothing okay about this. However, I do understand his battle with depression. I don't just say that as a cliché. I suffered from severe depression for many years. Almost no one knew. Like him, I was good at hiding it (well, y'all know now). ... It hurts me profoundly to the core that he couldn't make it over to 'the other side.' I was on that precipice. I feel lucky I have people in my life who kept me from taking that step off."[30]

STAMP OUT THE STIGMA

All of us can contribute to the end of the stigma associated with depression. Yes, strides have been made to eradicate the shame of depression from American society, but too many lives have been lost for us to continue this slow journey. More of us need to join the effort to educate the public about depression.

The responsibility for changing the negative perceptions about depression to a more benign view rests on all of us—family, friends, coworkers, acquaintances, and communities. "By learning about depression and passing the knowledge along, we can all help replace fear and rejection with understanding and respect."[31]

As human beings, we must help each other to better understand this disease. Education is the key to learning the facts about the illness and rising above the stigma it currently has. Once depression is understood by the masses, society can help itself by making information and resources available so no one has to suffer like I and others have over the centuries.

Depression Can Affect Anyone

When famous people speak out about their own struggles with depressive disorders, it goes a long way to removing the stigma of the disease. Here is a partial list of famous people throughout history who have struggled with depression.[32]

John Adams,* second president of the United States
Buzz Aldrin, American astronaut
Hans Christian Andersen,* Danish children's author
Roseanne Barr, comedian
Ludwig van Beethoven,* German composer
Ingmar Bergman, Swedish film director
Beyoncé, American singer
Terry Bradshaw, former Pittsburgh Steelers quarterback
Marlon Brando, actor

Barbara Bush, former first lady of the United States
Truman Capote, American writer
Jim Carrey, actor and comedian
Johnny Carson, American television host
Agatha Christie, English mystery writer
Winston Churchill, former British Prime Minister
Calvin Coolidge, thirtieth president of the United States
Sheryl Crow, singer
John Daly, professional golfer
Charles Darwin,* British naturalist
Diana, Princess of Wales
Charles Dickins,* English author
Emily Dickinson,* American poet
Lady Gaga, American singer-songwriter
Ernest Hemingway, Pulitzer Prize–winning novelist
Audrey Hepburn, British actress
Samuel Johnson,* British lexicographer
Stephen King, American novelist
Abraham Lincoln, sixteenth president of the United States
Mary Todd Lincoln, former first lady of the United States
Greg Louganis, American Olympic medal–winning diver
Michelangelo,* Italian painter and sculptor
Marilyn Monroe, American actress
Wolfgang Amadeus Mozart,* Austrian composer
Sir Isaac Newton,* English scientist
Friedrich Nietzsche,* German philosopher
Edgar Allan Poe, American poet and writer
John D. Rockefeller, American industrialist
Charles Spurgeon, English preacher
Leo Tolstoy, Russian novelist
Mark Twain, American writer
Vincent van Gogh,* Impressionist painter
Robin Williams, American actor and comedian
Oprah Winfrey, American talk show host
Boris Yeltsin, first president of Russia

*Historical research supports these persons as having suffered from some form of depression.

Chapter 3

Depression's Impact on Children, Teens, and College Students

"A big part of depression is feeling really lonely, even if you're in a room full of a million people."

—Lilly Singh, Canadian comedian

DEPRESSION THROWS TURMOIL INTO THE LIVES OF CHILDREN, teens, and young adults who suffer from it. During a season of life when they're growing and their brains are developing, it is particularly stressful for youth to struggle with depression. "We need to understand that depression in youth looks differently," says Deborahanne Reimer, a licensed clinical professional counselor certified in alcohol and drug counseling who works with youth at a Chicago, Illinois, high school. "Depression in youth often manifests as irritability and anger, which is easily overlooked as typical teenage behavior."[33]

Caring parents, teachers, coaches, and others who recognize signs of depression in the youth they know can reach out to help. Children, teens, and college students who get the diagnoses and treatment they need can enter adulthood with a stronger foundation, prepared to launch their lives as adults without being crippled by the disease.

Although youth may seem like a carefree time, it's also a time when many people are afflicted by depression. "About 5 percent of children and adolescents in the general population suffer from depression at any given point in time," according to the American Academy of Child & Adolescent Psychiatry. "Children under stress, who experience loss, or who have attentional, learning, conduct or anxiety disorders are at a higher risk for depression. Depression also tends to run in families."[34]

The older youth become, it seems, the more likely they are to start experiencing depression. "Depression occurs at a rate of about 2% during childhood and from 4%–7% during adolescence,"[35] MedicineNet.com says. The article adds that "depression is common during the teenage years, affecting about 20% of adolescents by the time they reach adulthood."[36]

"There's been an actual increase in depression in emerging adults (those between the ages of 18 and 29)," says Dr. Crystal I. Lee, a licensed psychologist and owner of LA Concierge Psychologist in Los Angeles, California. "With my clients and from research, usage of Instagram, Facebook, and other social media correlates with more depressive symptoms and decreased overall mental health."[37]

According to the National Institute of Mental Health, "in 2015, an estimated 3 million adolescents aged 12 to 17 in the United States had at least one major depressive episode in the past year. This number represented 12.5 percent of the U.S. population aged 12 to 17."[38] Contrast that with the statistics for depression among adults age 18 years and older "In 2015, an estimated 16.1 million adults aged 18 or older in the United States had at least one major depressive episode in the past year. This number represented 6.7 percent of all U.S. adults."[39] A greater percentage of the adolescent population suffers from depression than the adult population (including college students) does.

A recent study of depression among teen girls showed that "depression in many children appears to start as early as age 11. By the time they hit age 17, the analysis found, 13.6 percent of boys and a staggering 36.1 percent of girls have been or are depressed. These numbers are significantly higher than previous estimates."[40]

It makes sense for adults who are concerned about the youth they love to pay close attention when those young people seem depressed, and to intervene to help when needed. "As much as we've made strides—significant strides in mental health issues—there's still quite a bit of stigma and stain surrounding all of that," says Dr. Lee. "A lot of the clients I work with start to isolate from others, which feeds depression and anxiety, because of the shame of experiencing depressive symptoms. The more we can encourage those who need help to get help, the better quality of life they will experience."

DEPRESSIVE TRIGGERS

While the suspected causes of depression at any age are complex—and range from chemical imbalances in people's brains to stress in their environment—some risk factors seem to contribute to depression among youth. They include the stress of change and uncertainty, changes in developing brains, and substance abuse.

Young people frequently experience change in their lives, and they're often uncertain about what will happen to them as a result of that change. Youth is a season of growth that is characterized by change—from different school and extracurricular activities to various friendships—as children, teens, and young adults learn more about who they are as people and discover what they want to do with their lives. Questions and uncertainty abound during this season of life, as youth shape their personal identities.

"The increase in social media, the decrease in authentic conversations, and the loud voice in their heads, plus everyone's expectations and ideas of what 'happy' is has fed into clinical depression among our youth," says Lynn R Zakeri, LCSW, in private practice in the Chicago, Illinois, area. "There's always been sadness but now we hear about it a lot more."[41]

All that change and uncertainty may lead to depression, especially among young adults. LiveScience.com says: "Young adults are saying goodbye to childhood and adolescence, and trying to make their own way while dealing with frequent change and uncertainty, which could trigger feelings of sadness and irritability. Going off into the world, establishing a clear identity, developing a capacity for intimate relationships, and forming a foundation to build a future career and adult life are all part of the challenges to people in their twenties that could make them vulnerable to depression, said Dr. Stuart Goldman, a child and adolescent psychiatrist at Boston Children's Hospital."[42]

The stress of both personal and professional changes may contribute to young adults developing depression, according to an article from Child Trends/DataBank Indicator. "Young adulthood, defined here as between the ages of 18 and 29, is a time of great change for many people, and has been associated with greater risk of mental health problems and higher levels of social stress."[43]

"Many of today's emerging adults have no resiliency, and have been thrust into a more stressful environment without coping skills," says Dr. Lee. "That's another reason why we're seeing more mental health issues with college students."

Some of those changes include starting to work in unrewarding jobs and dealing with the challenges of getting married and starting families. "Unemployment and unrewarding job environments, such as those characterized by few low-level cognitive demands, minimal skills, and little autonomy (common features of many entry-level jobs), have been linked with depression among young adults,"[44] the article says. In addition, it states: "While positive aspects of marriage often serve to protect against depression, new financial burdens, career demands, a poor adjustment to married life, and the birth of children among young couples can also lead to negative mental health outcomes, especially among women."[45]

Brain development that happens during the teen and early adult years has also been identified as a possible cause of depression when the disease is somehow triggered during the maturation process. As LiveScience.com says: "those in their early 20s are dealing with these challenges before their brain is fully mature. The prefrontal cortex—the part of the brain involved in reasoning and controlling—finishes developing about age 25. Most people who have a genetic vulnerability to depression, typically experience their first episode of the condition between ages 14 and 24."[46]

Substance abuse—especially involving alcohol, cigarettes, and opioid drugs—also seems to be a risk factor for depression among youth. The Child Trends/DataBank Indicator article states that, "young adulthood coincides with the legal age for alcohol use. Young adults who engage in frequent drinking, or who smoke cigarettes, are more likely to experience depression."[47]

"Teens and young adults turn to alcohol to self-medicate," says Reimer. "Often in college, drinking alcohol is overlooked as a symptom of depression because of the perception that everybody drinks in college. Our culture has created this disguise that hides identifying the problem of depression, and substance abuse is often used as a band-aid."

Opioid addiction, an epidemic in the United States, has also been linked to depression as a possible cause of the disease.

Opioids are often prescribed to control pain. Youth who may at first take an opioid medication for pain relief (such as while recovering from an injury) may become addicted to that medication and continue to take it on a long-term basis. By doing so, they may make themselves vulnerable to depression.

As a PsychCentral.com article says, "New research suggests that while opioids may cause a short-term improvement in mood, long-term use increases the chance of depression."[48] That article refers to research from Saint Louis University, noting that "long-term opioid use of more than 30 days can lead to changes in neuroanatomy and low testosterone, among other possible biological explanations."[49] Further, "the relationship between opioid drugs and depression was independent of the known contribution of pain to depression. Accordingly, the study calls on clinicians to consider the contribution of opioid use when depressed mood develops in their patients."[50]

The good news is that some factors appear to help protect youth from developing depression. According to MedicineNet.com, "protective factors for teen depression include having the involvement of supportive adults, strong family and peer relationships, healthy coping skills, and skills in emotion regulation."[51]

HOME CONTRIBUTIONS

When children experience persistent lonely feelings, those emotions may make them more vulnerable to developing depression than kids who enjoy loving relationships with friends and family. When parents fail to provide a warm, caring environment for children at home, their kids may also be more prone to depression than those who feel cared for well at home. "Children who struggle with ongoing loneliness may be ... more likely to be sad, disconnected and worried. ... These negative feelings combined with continued isolation can lead to depression and anxiety."[52]

A recent study of adolescent girls who were involved in child welfare agency cases found that lonely youth were likely to be depressed, depressed youth were likely to be lonely, and youth who experienced depression and/or loneliness were likely to be falling behind in school and lacking hope for their future. These "findings suggest that there are statistically significant and fairly substantial bidirectional relationships between loneliness and depression or depression-related factors that include school disengagement and low expectations for the future."[53]

Depressed adults who didn't receive enough emotional support from their parents growing up may have been affected by that lack of support in a way that contributed to them developing depression later, another study revealed. Researchers at the University of Albany and the University of Michigan "found a lack of parental support during childhood is associated with increased levels of depressive symptoms and chronic health conditions (such as hypertension, arthritis, and urinary problems) in adulthood, and this association persists with increasing age throughout adulthood into early old age."[54]

These connections between loneliness and depression show the importance of parents, teachers, and other caring adults reaching out to youth who seem lonely. The study of adolescent girls advised several ways that parents and other caring adults can intervene to try to help lonely young people: "In order to help prevent depression, school disengagement, or low expectations for the future, a variety of interventions can address loneliness. Such interventions include enhancing peer or family relationships, for example, or promoting participation in prosocial activities (e.g., sports, clubs at school, youth groups in the community). These network-enhancing strategies can help to introduce or develop potentially close connections that prevent or counteract loneliness in order to avert depression or depression-related factors."[55]

Loving parents are especially important to help prevent depression. A University of California–Los Angeles (UCLA) study suggests that relationships between parents may alter neural circuits in children that affect their health throughout their lifetimes—including their risk of developing depression. Emotionally cold parent-child relationships led to a greater risk of mental and physical health problems for the children, while loving parent-child relationships led to better health.[56]

Findings point out "that a loving relationship may also prevent the rise in biomarkers indicative of disease risk across numerous physiological systems, impacting adverse health outcomes decades later. ... The UCLA findings suggest that parental warmth and affection protect one against the harmful effects of toxic childhood stress."[57]

HELICOPTER PARENTING

Helicopter parents—those who are either overprotective of their children or excessively involved in their children's lives—intend to try to protect their children from suffering. Ironically, though, helicopter parents often end up achieving the exact opposite: causing unnecessary suffering for their children. A tragic example of this is the link between helicopter parenting and depression. "College-aged students whose parents are overly involved in their academic lives, or whose parents created rigidly structured childhood environments, are more likely to experience anxiety and depression. ... They may also experience academic difficulties."[58]

Kirsten Li-Barber, assistant professor of psychology at High Point University in North Carolina, discussed research that shows helicopter parenting may contribute to depression in a ChicagoTribune.com article: "Research of teens with overprotective parents ... has found they are more anxious, less socially skilled, have poorer coping skills and higher rates of depression. In addition, they don't transition to college well."[59]

How can helicopter parenting lead to depression in youth? The answer seems to be by squelching young people's developmental needs to build competence through autonomy. A study of college students revealed that "students who reported having over-controlling parents reported significantly higher levels of depression and less satisfaction with life. Furthermore, the negative effects of helicopter parenting on college students' well-being were largely explained by the perceived violation of students' basic psychological needs for autonomy and competence. ... Lower levels of competence were related to higher levels of depression and lower levels of satisfaction with life. Additionally, lower perceived autonomy was associated with more depression. More specifically, helicopter behaviors were shown to have significant indirect effects on both depression and life satisfaction through competence as well as an indirect effect on depression through autonomy."[60]

The study elaborated on the process, noting that "students who feel as if they are being 'helicoptered' also feel that their basic psychological needs are not being met. When parents engage in controlling behaviors, students' sense of personal autonomy may be diminished. Feeling a lack of volition and control can lead to depression."[61]

In her book *How to Raise an Adult: Break Free of the Overparenting Trap and Prepare Your Kid for Success*, Julie Lythcott-Haims commented that "the research shows that figuring out for themselves is a critical element to people's mental health. Your kids have to be there for *themselves*. That's a harder truth to swallow when your kid is in the midst of a problem or worse, a crisis, but taking the long view, it's the best medicine for them."[62]

Helicopter parents who want to change their ways to reduce the risk of their children developing depression can simply start choosing to pull back as their kids grow older. "Parenting experts say you need to imprint solid values—like honesty and a work ethic—and then get out of the way when your children become teenagers, grow up, and start making their own decisions—and deal with the consequences, for better or worse."[63]

YOUTH DEPRESSION SIGNS

Behaviors that may be signs of depression in young people mirror common signs of adult depression: Sad or irritable feelings, fatigue, and social isolation that persist for more than two weeks and interfere with a person's ability to function normally. But other potential signs of depression are distinctively symptoms for youth.

Children who are depressed may show signs that include diminished performance in school, unsafe play behaviors (such as running into a street while playing), crying frequently, angry outbursts, problems sleeping or eating well, unexplained bodily complaints (like headaches that don't have a known physical cause), and persistent boredom, notes MedicineNet.com.[64] Additional signs of depression in children include talking about or acting on efforts to run away from home, and a loss of enjoyment in activities that a child had previously enjoyed, according to the American Academy of Child & Adolescent Psychiatry.[65]

Reimer also points to irritability and anger as depressive symptoms specifically in children and adolescents. "Parents usually think their teen is being moody, and can minimize the symptoms as being part of the normal teen's life," she says. "Parents can watch out for changes in routines or friends, isolating and spending too much time online or in their room, and alcohol or drug use."

Teens and young adults who are depressed may also exhibit signs like these in addition to the classic symptoms of depression: Dropping grades at school, using or increasing use of alcohol and/or drugs, unhealthy eating or sleeping patterns, weight gain or loss, loneliness, and expressing hopelessness or a fixation on past failures, according to MentalHealthTreatment.net.[66] Other signs of depression in teens and young adults include driving recklessly and engaging in promiscuous or unprotected sex, MedicineNet.com says.[67]

For college students, depressive symptoms can masquerade as typical university life. "Watch out for sleeping in too much or insomnia in your student," cautions Dr. Lee. She also suggests asking questions like:

- Am I irritable because I'm stressed or starting to develop depression?
- Am I tearful because of the friend drama or legitimately depressed?
- Am I missing classes because I'm tired or because I can't sleep due to depression?

Zakeri emphasizes how important sleep is to a healthy mind and body. "Sleep is the number one thing to staying healthy, so if you're not getting the right kind of sleep or sleeping too much that can create a pattern of unhealthy thoughts, which can exacerbate or lead to depression," she says.

YOUTH DEPRESSION TREATMENT

Depressed youth and their parents often turn to counseling therapy to treat the disease, and sometimes combine therapy with prescription medication. "Comprehensive treatment often includes both individual and family therapy," says the American Academy of Child & Adolescent Psychiatry. For example, cognitive behavioral therapy (CBT) and interpersonal psychotherapy (IPT) are forms of individual therapy shown to be effective in treating depression. Treatment may also include the use of anti-depressant medication."[68]

"What I find is a preference not to jump straight into medication, but to try talk therapy first, then consider medications if necessary," says Reimer. "It's important to help youth and young adults to learn the skills to identify and self-manage their emotions."

The Mayo Clinic explains how therapy and medication may work to effectively treat depression in young patients: "Most children who take antidepressants for depression will improve with medication. However, combining medication with talk therapy (psychotherapy) is likely to be even more effective. Many types of psychotherapy may be helpful, but cognitive behavioral therapy and interpersonal therapy have been scientifically studied and shown to be effective for treating depression. ... For some children and teenagers with mild symptoms, talk therapy alone may be beneficial."[69]

Cognitive behavioral therapy involves learning coping, communication, and problem-solving skills to manage emotions. Interpersonal therapy involves adapting to stress in relationships and building healthier relationships when possible.

For college students, universities have counseling centers that can assist with assessments of mental health, including depression, and can help guide students to finding qualified counselors and doctors. "I always encourage students to go to their school's counseling center for an assessment when they're unsure if it's sadness or depression they are experiencing," says Zakeri.

When youth take medication to treat depression, they are often prescribed antidepressants that adults take, but in smaller doses. Those antidepressant drugs include Escitalopram (Lexapro), Fluoxetine (Prozac), and Olanzapine and Fluoxetine (Symbyax), as well as their generic versions.[70]

Antidepressants can successfully treat depression in young patients, but they should be monitored carefully because they may sometimes raise the risk of suicide in youth whose brains are still developing. "Antidepressant drugs are often an effective way to treat depression and anxiety in children and teenagers. However, antidepressant use in children and teens must be monitored carefully, as rarely there can be severe side effects. Antidepressants carry a Food and Drug Administration (FDA) black box warning about a risk of increased suicidal thinking and behavior in some individuals under the age of 25."[71]

The Mayo Clinic advises parents and health-care professionals to monitor youth for any suicidal thoughts or behaviors during transition times of being on antidepressant drugs: "The highest risk of suicidal thinking and behavior occurs: During the first few months of treatment with an antidepressant [and] when the dosage is increased or decreased."[72]

EARLY INTERVENTION

While the ways to treat depression in youth are much the same as they are to treat the disease in adults, it's especially important to act on treatment for young patients, because early intervention may stop depression from becoming more severe in their lives. Researcher Elizabeth Miller, director of the division of adolescent medicine at Children's Hospital of Pittsburgh, makes that point: "When you are seeing young people with symptoms consistent with depression it is really much, much better to get them connected to a pediatrician to get them a comprehensive mental health assessment and hook them into treatment sooner rather than later."[73] The American Academy of Child & Adolescent Psychiatry also urges that, "Early diagnosis and treatment are essential for depressed children."[74]

Another vital reason to treat depression in young people as soon as possible is because doing so may help prevent other problems to which youth depression may lead. As MedicineNet.com explains, "teens with depression are more likely to engage in self-mutilation. ... Adolescents with depression are also at risk of having poor school performance, early pregnancy, and engaging in alcohol and other drug abuse. As adults, people who suffered from depression during adolescence are at risk for job disruptions, as well as family and other social upheaval during adulthood."[75] Child Trends/DataBank Indicator says that "depression in adolescence is associated with higher levels of depression and poorer health outcome in young adulthood. Young adults who suffer from depression are more likely to have problems with psychological functioning, interpersonal relationships, employment, and substance abuse, and to be more dissatisfied with life. They also show higher rates of absenteeism from work."[76]

Suicide, which is linked to depression, is a leading cause of death among youth. So it's wise to treat depression in young people before the disease increases their risk of killing themselves. The American Academy of Child & Adolescent Psychiatry warns that "depressed children and adolescents are at increased risk for committing suicide."[77] Clinical depression "is a leading cause of health impairment (morbidity) and death (mortality)," notes MedicineNet.com. "About three thousand adolescents and young adults die by suicide each year in the United States, making it the third leading cause of death in people [10 to 24] years of age."[78]

A PARENT'S PERSPECTIVE

For parents, seeing your child suffer from depression can fill you with emotions. "Parents often feel helpless themselves," says Zakeri. "It's really hard to help someone who's hurting, but parents have to be the older/wiser grownup, to be the one to say, 'let's find out how we can get some help with this,' or 'let's look to other people to handle this.'"

Parents often respond with initial disbelief and denial, believing that depression is not a real disease—that if they minimize it, it will go away. "I tell parents that if your child had cancer, then you would immediately contact a medical professional and insist on treatment," says Reimer. "It should be the same with depression."

How can parents help? By talking to their child. "I recommend parents approach the topic in a safe, nonjudgmental way, with more empathy, by asking questions like, 'how are you doing?'" says Zakeri. "There are apps like iMood that can help people figure out what they're feeling, for example, much like the pain scale doctors and hospitals use."

When parents reach out to medical professionals for guidance or to make appointments for their offspring, "they should start with someone who specializes in mental health, like psychologists, psychiatrists, and licensed mental health professionals," says Reimer.

Parents can encourage their college students to utilize the resources available on campus. "The college counseling center can determine if you have depression, give referrals for medical professionals, and provide other guidance to help the student improve their quality of life," says Dr. Lee. "However, it can be difficult for parents to recognize their limitations if an emerging adult doesn't want to seek help."

As we continue to remove barriers to treatment and the stigma surrounding mental illness, more youth struggling with depression will find hope. "Depression is a medical disease that's common and treatable," reminds Reimer. "By giving parents and youth hope that this is a manageable situation, by empowering them to seek treatment, and by educating them about the disease, we can help more children, teens, and college students recover from depression and live full lives."

Chapter 4

Depression's Impact on Patients

"Depression isn't about, 'Woe is me, my life is this, that, and the other;' it's like having the worst flu all day that you just can't kick."
—Robbie Williams, English singer-songwriter

WHAT IS DEPRESSION? DOCTORS CAN GIVE YOU A MEDICAL AND biological analysis of what happens in your brain if you have depression, but for most people, that level of detail can be hard to follow. My first psychopharmacologist provided the following layman's description of depression that I've found to be very helpful in my understanding of the disease:

What is happening in my brain? In your brain, you have brain cells. These cells are connected by synapses or pathways between cells. When you are depressed, these synapses or pathways are closed. The medication opens the pathways so your normal brain chemicals—the ones that make you feel good—can flow normally. The meds don't change who you are; rather, they let you be who you are.

Today, technology has given us tools to diagnose depression. In August 2017, Google unveiled a new feature for U.S. users who search for "clinical depression" or "depression"—a short questionnaire they can take to test their levels of depression to assist in determining whether professional help is needed. "The clinically validated test, called PHQ-9, asks about energy, appetite, and concentration levels, among other things."[79]

Google developed the initiative with the National Alliance on Mental Illness (NAMI), and said it would not store responses to the questionnaire. "The results of the PHQ-9 can help you have a more informed conversation with your doctor," said Mary Giliberti, CEO of NAMI. "We hope that by making this information available on Google, more people will become aware of depression and seek treatment to recover and improve their quality of life."[80]

It can often be difficult for depressed people to view medication in this way because of potential side effects. With cancer, for instance, the patient might feel physically incapacitated, but can see the need for the often painful or distressing treatment, and therefore steels himself to go the distance even when he wants to give up.

Another challenge in treating depression is that if the person has cycled out of depression in the past and has another episode, what worked in the past might not work again or work in the same way. During my fourth bout of depression (13 years ago), my doctors prescribed the same medications that had brought me out of previous depressions, but those didn't work this time. The cycle of trying different combinations and dosages made the depression episode more prolonged and drawn out. My ruminations became even stranger, and my relationship with a woman with three children became unsustainable and ended abruptly.

By this point, I had been fighting depression for two years and wasn't in good shape at all. I was sorry the relationship ended, but I was very sick and needed to focus all my energy on getting better. Experts advise people who are depressed not to be in or maybe not to start a new relationship (unless you're married, of course), and not to make any major decisions.

Because depression is not viewed in the same vein as cancer or other diseases of the body, it can be difficult for those who suffer from it to have the support of their communities and families. If we could normalize depression even more, we could lower the rate of suicide and offer more hope to those who have the disease. We should be more willing to help the person during his or her depressive episodes, and understand that it's an illness like many illnesses we now know aren't necessarily caused by the patient, such as diabetes and heart disease.

Chapter 5

Depression's Impact on Families

"Here is the tragedy: When you are the victim of depression, not only do you feel utterly helpless and abandoned by the world, you also know that very few people can understand, or even begin to believe, that life can be this painful."
—Giles Andreae, English artist and poet

THOSE SUFFERING FROM DEPRESSION OFTEN FACE DIFFICULTIES within their own families, because the disease is still so very misunderstood. Family members' reactions can help or hinder that person's treatment. Family members also are challenged when they know a person needs help, but are helpless to push him or her into treatment. Other times family members can grow weary of interacting with someone in the throes of a deep depression. Although it's never easy for the depressed person, it can be just as difficult for the family members of someone with depression.

My mother is a good example. Although now she realizes that the illness does run in our family, in the beginning she was in denial of her own depression, which first started after her parents died. Prior to that, my mom led a happy, fun life. Her depressions seemed to trigger when there was someone in the family dealing with health problems or a death in the immediate family. She doesn't like doctors, so she wasn't helpful in seeking assistance for her depression. "We're watching it very closely because my grandmother had depression, my father had it, and others in the family did too," says my mother, Dona Litzsinger.[81]

My father didn't understand the disease when I was younger either. He had difficulty dealing with my mother and the disease because they didn't really talk about it or tell us kids what was going on. It was one of those hidden things that no one talked about because no one knew exactly what it was. And my mother didn't always want the treatments available at the time because of various side effects. Society at that time viewed depression as a "mental breakdown" (a quite horrific term), and people didn't talk about it with extended family, much less friends or the public because of the stigma.

With depression, patients sometimes go years without a diagnosis, and often don't even realize this "blue feeling" has a potential cure. Sometimes the person doesn't want to admit they have or could have depression. I saw firsthand how that denial can impact a person as my mother didn't acknowledge her own depression diagnoses in the beginning. Of course, back then, we didn't have medication or treatments like we do now, but watching her suffer—even though I didn't know what to call it—made me determined to get help for my own depression.

That's a huge part of the disease—this hiding it, being afraid to talk about it while you're going through it because you don't think people will understand the illness. At the executive level, I've often thought there are probably a lot of executives who have some type of depression who can't talk about it—or think they can't talk about it. They're afraid that if they do talk about it or acknowledge they are depressed, it may affect their career. I know I was concerned about that.

Dr. Norman Bengtsten was the first psychiatrist to diagnose my illness. Dr. Bengtsten and his wife were my grandparents' best friends, and we all called him Uncle Norman. I reached out to Norman when I didn't know what to do about how bad I was feeling mentally. He diagnosed me with depression within 15 minutes of our appointment, then told me that he had treated my grandfather, mother, and others in my mom's family. "The good thing was, unlike many people who were depressed in those days, Mark wanted to try to do something about it," remembers my father. "Mark was willing to learn about depression and not consider it some bad thing people were not willing to talk about."

DEPRESSION ON THE OUTSIDE

For those close to someone with depression, deciphering which part of the person is the disease and which is his or her true self can be hard at times. Sometimes those with depression do a better job of hiding the disease behind a more bubbly public persona. For example, my sister Robin, the second of our five siblings, was initially quite surprised to find out about my depression. "Mark was such a happy-go-lucky person, very sociable and involved in high school and college," she says. "I always looked up to him as my older brother and especially when boys came into the picture. He was a normal, happy, upper-middle-class, privileged-type person with no real problems."[82]

"The signs of depression were weird for Mark, and they didn't start out all at once but were gradual," adds my father. "During one of his major depression episodes, he was chairman of our company and things progressed where it was almost embarrassing because of Mark's lack of concentration and his serious issues with guilt—beyond what was normal and that rendered him unable to let go of and move on from specific incidents."

My younger sister, Heidi Baumann, the third child in our family, wasn't surprised by my depression diagnosis because of our mother's illness. "I think my mother and her depression issues were really hard on Mark because of him being the oldest," says Heidi.[83]

Shawn Stratman, the fourth sibling, says she always knew when I was struggling with depression. "He would ruminate and ask a lot of questions, the same questions over and over again. I'd talk to him about it, but he would go back to the same thing over and over to the point that it was exhausting when he would call," Shawn says. "But, of course, you take the call and do your very best to give him something to hold onto overnight. It was clearly bothering him and he would be up all night worrying about it, something he might have said, something he had done, something that he may have forgotten. There were just so many details to everything he was doing and he struggled with it."[84]

With eight years between Shawn and myself, she and I didn't become very close until some of my later depressive episodes. "That's when our relationship really grew—when I was a grown woman and he was battling this," she recalls. "Mark could hide his depression during an episode for short periods of time. He could pull himself together, but it would be a struggle."

My brother, Todd Litzsinger, the youngest in our family, had a different experience, partly because of our 10-year age difference. "Mark in his depression would describe things over and over, even minor issues that he couldn't let go," says Todd, adding that he idolized me as his older brother. "He's a very truthful and honest person, but the depression made him increasingly paranoid and overly concerned about doing right and avoiding wrong."[85]

KNOWLEDGE IS UNDERSTANDING

My own family's reactions and interactions during my depression episodes underscored to me the importance of family members' understanding the disease as much as possible in order to support their loved ones during their journey out of depression. Here are some things families should be aware of when a member has been diagnosed with depression:

- **Risk factor.** "Family members should know a couple of things when someone in their family has been diagnosed with depression," says Dr. Scheftner. "The number one is that they too are at risk for depression, because if you have one member of the family with depression, your chances of identifying another member of the family with depression probably doubles."

- **Expectations.** Everyone reacts to depression treatment differently—what works for one person might not work for another. Family members need to be aware of that and adjust their expectations accordingly. "Part of that adjustment is the fact that someone being treated for depression will still have bad days," explains Dr. Mark Pollack,[86] chairman of the Department of Psychiatry at Rush University Medical Center in Chicago, Illinois. Sometimes people expect the treatment to kick in right away, but that doesn't usually happen. Medications can take weeks to show results. (See Chapter 18 for more on what family members should know about depression treatment.)

- **Compassion.** When a person goes through depression, they can be in a fog at times, even when getting treatment. "My sister Heidi and I helped Mark during his last major depression. We went with him to ECT [electroconvulsive or shock therapy] treatments and brought him home afterwards to make sure he got sleep, ate, etc. It was eye-opening as a sibling to watch what happened to him," says Robin.

- **Patience.** For some with depression, recovery can take years, which can really wear on family members. Other times, the particular manifestation of the depression can stretch their limits. "For me, it was Mark's obsessive-compulsive disorder and ruminating. It was hard to hear the same thing over and over and over, day after day without any change," says Robin. "No matter how many times you told Mark to move past it, he couldn't get beyond it. It was really hard." During those periods, she stresses how important it was for her to recognize it was the disease talking and not her brother.

- **Support.** It's important for all family members to be as supportive as they can during the patient's treatment and recovery. That helps to provide the patient with the foundation on which to build his or her recovery. The support can be as low-key as phone calls to check in with the patient or as hands-on as driving the person to treatment and bringing him or her home afterwards. "Depression treatment is time-consuming and frustrating because it can go on and on and on," says my father. "That's why family support is so critical to the patient."

Support also can come in the form of helping the person cope at work while battling depression. Todd worked with me at our family company during my worst depression, which started when I was 47 and lasted two years. "Mark would get on these tangents over things that weren't as big as he was making them out to be, and it became very clear that something was wrong," says Todd. "He really went into this depression where I and my cousin at work tried to keep things going, to distract everybody else to prevent people from noticing certain things about Mark's behavior."

- **Professional help.** Encourage your family member to get help through the best medical care available. I highly recommend seeking psychiatric care at a teaching hospital if possible. "You need to get them to a professional who can analyze and start the process. That's the first thing they should do. Don't wait around for it to cure itself, because it could get worse. And I doubt it will cure itself," says my father.

A CHANGING WORLD?

We hope that the world is changing, that depression won't be as stigmatized or marginalized as it has been in the past. Having family members who understand depression is essential to recovery. "You have to both understand what depression is and that there are ways to get professional help, that there can be a light at the end of the tunnel," notes my father.

Part of the problem with depression is that we use the term generically. There are actually two types of depression: situational depression and genetic depression. Depression is like a final common pathway that patients can develop as a result of genetic or other biologic vulnerabilities, life events and stressors, cognitive style or some combination of those. With genetic depression, a person is genetically predisposed to have a chemical imbalance. "When you really wrap your mind around that, my desire is that we would address it as genetic depression, which would be what Mark and our family carry—a true genetic disease— and situational depression, which is incidental, onset depression where something happens, and your body and mind respond with depression," says Shawn. She stresses that making this distinction will help family members assist their loved one through the depression with more compassion and understanding.

Families play a large part in a person's recovery from depression. "I don't think anyone can come out of depression without someone helping them," says my mother. My father adds, "I think Mark's recovery has been so remarkable because of the huge role his siblings played in helping him. They are all super kids and really care about each other. They all came together and did what they could to be supportive of Mark, more than he probably realized."

Part II
The Doctors

Chapter 6

Doctors and Depression

"The best thing you can do to make your depression treatment a success is to find a doctor who will work with you and whom you can trust."
— Dr. Wes Burgess, English author, in *The Depression Answer Book*

People suffering from depression can seek treatment for the disease from a variety of health-care professionals, including psychiatrists, psychologists, and social workers. Choosing the right type of provider is crucial for building a strong doctor/patient relationship that promotes healing.

Most people start the journey with their internist or primary-care physician. If you have classic depression symptoms, such as those listed on page 10 in Chapter 1, then your internist or primary-care doctor will likely refer you to a psychiatrist or psychologist. What I've found is that you as the patient often have to educate the educators because sometimes internists aren't up to speed on depression treatment. The internists or a psychiatrist could treat the depression and may be successful. However, someone like a psychopharmacologist—a psychiatrist who specializes in medication management—will provide a more focused regimen that will target your depression more thoroughly.

Sometimes treatment by a psychopharmacologist is combined with that of a talk therapist (see Chapter 13 for more on talk therapy and depression). A psychopharmacologist will go through a lot of material, such as a patient's full medical and family history, that might be relevant to the illness, especially if you have family members who have received a depression diagnosis and know what medications they tried.

The ultimate goal of the search for the right treatment is for patients to find health-care professionals who will partner with them throughout the healing process. "The two of you need to work as a team, making decisions, sharing information, and discussing the benefits and risks of different treatment options. It should be a two-way street with mutual participation in all decisions."[87]

THE ROLE OF PRIMARY-CARE DOCTORS

Patients will probably begin their search for the right health-care providers by asking their primary-care doctor questions that will help the patients find the right caregiver. After hearing the basic details about a patient's individual concerns about depression, a primary-care doctor can make recommendations and referrals to help develop an effective treatment plan.

Many primary-care physicians prescribe medications, such as antidepressants or sedatives, to patients with depression, but their experience with depression medications or depression treatment might be more limited. For example, primary-care doctors often have knowledge of one or two antidepressants, and can be "less rigorous in their diagnosis of depression than psychiatrists are."[88]

Health-care experts like the Mayo Clinic recommend asking for a doctor referral from a patient's primary-care doctor. Additional potential sources of therapist referrals or recommendations include health insurance companies, friends, family members, clergy, and professional mental health associations.[89]

THE ROLE OF PSYCHOPHARMACOLOGY

One key question for depressed people to consider when searching for the right health-care professional is whether or not they would like to try medication to treat their disease. Many medical professionals who treat depression are also psychopharmacologists who use medications and psychology to treat mental disorders.

Depressed patients should educate themselves about the psychopharmacology of any drugs they're considering taking. It can be helpful to ask their doctors basic psychopharmacology questions such as:

- How will the medication work in my body?
- How long will the medication stay in my body?
- Will other medications I'm currently taking interact with this medication, and if so, how?

Any medical doctor who can prescribe drugs to treat mental conditions (like depression) must be thoroughly educated in psychopharmacology. "In a generic sense, any physician who treats patients with psychotropic medication is a psychopharmacologist.... Physicians who have completed residency training after medical school have a high level of understanding and expertise in pharmacology, including psychopharmacology. Psychiatrists (who have completed four years of advanced training after medical school) have an even higher level of understanding and expertise in psychopharmacology."[90]

Once patients decide to pursue medications to treat their depression, they also should consider what the definitive goal is of using those medications. The most helpful goal may be to combine medications with therapy in strategic ways as psycho-pharmacology has been found to be more effective when com-bined with psychotherapy. "Yes, taking medication at some point may be a crucial part of the patient's responsibility for getting better, but it is no substitute for real psychotherapy. How psy-chopharmacology and its implicit psychology is understood and employed in psychotherapy is key: Is medication used merely to deaden metaphorical demons? Or to support confronting and coming to terms with them?"[91]

THE ROLE OF PSYCHIATRISTS

Psychiatrists are the most experienced of the health-care pro-fessionals who treat depression. Basically, a psychiatrist diagno-ses, counsels, treats, and prescribes medication for those with mental-health disorders.

Many times psychiatrists are the best option for depression treatment. "Compared with other professionals, they usually have the most experience treating patients with severe depres-sion. In addition to their understanding of the wealth of medica-tions used to treat unipolar major depression, psychiatrists are the only medical doctors who are fully trained in psychotherapy for depression. ... They should be able to discuss all the relevant benefits, side effects, and risks of whatever treatment you choose. They may offer to do both medications and psychotherapy to-gether in the same session."[92]

The drawback is that psychiatrists also are usually the most expensive type of doctor who treats depression. The Mayo Clinic advises patients to check the details of their health-insurance policies or other health coverage (like Medicare or Medicaid) when researching potential treatment options so they can make informed decisions. But for those who can afford it, getting depression treatment from psychiatrists may be best for patients with severe depression. "In general, the more severe your symptoms or complex your diagnosis, the more expertise and training you need to look for in a mental health provider."[93]

THE ROLE OF PSYCHOLOGISTS

Psychologists are not medical doctors like psychiatrists, so they can't prescribe antidepressant drugs unless they have a special license. However, they do receive extensive training in how to treat depression. A psychologist diagnoses and treats many mental-health disorders, and provides psychological counseling in group settings or individually.

The training for psychologists involves earning a doctoral degree (a PhD) and completing a year of practical internship. "They may be the only sources for behavioral or cognitive psychotherapy in your community. Professional psychologists do not receive extensive training in the biology or pharmacology of depression in the brain and nervous system. Professional psychologists' fees are usually less than psychiatrists' fees and more than counselors' fees."[94]

Psychologists can be experts at treating depression through counseling therapy, but usually refer their patients who need antidepressant medication to other health-care providers like physicians, physician assistants, and nurses who can prescribe and monitor drug therapy in conjunction with the counseling they provide. This means many patients with depression may need more than one doctor to assist in managing their illness—one for counseling and one for prescribing medications.

Most state laws restrict prescription writing to medical doctors only. "A few states have given doctoral psychologists the ability to prescribe a few drugs, but they do not receive the extensive training in human biology and psychopharmacology that is provided to medical doctors."[95]

THE ROLE OF SOCIAL WORKERS

Social workers who are trained to help evaluate and treat depression also can help patients through counseling. In addition, social workers often deal with the broad scope of lifestyle changes that promote healing in depressed patients' lives. So if depressed people want help with general life issues—such as advice on how to improve family relationships or help managing time and energy in healthier ways—social workers can provide that assistance. In addition, social workers can be valuable resources for patients who want help accessing services from large organizations like hospitals or government agencies.

The social workers who treat mental health conditions such as depression "provide assessment, psychological counseling, and a range of other services, depending on their licensing and training; are not licensed to prescribe medication [and] may work with another provider who can prescribe medication if needed."[96]

Social workers also can help patients navigate federal, state, and local services available to those with depression and their families. Often, social workers have training in family psychotherapy. "Licensed clinical social workers (LCSWs) have extra training in psychotherapy and mental illness. Some social workers provide service at low or deferred cost."[97]

Wherever you begin your journey, finding the right doctor to guide you on your way to recovery might take some time. My advice is to go to the top of the food chain when it comes to finding help for depression, and psychopharmacologists are at the top. Unfortunately, many people suffering from depression haven't had access to a psychopharmacologist, either because they didn't realize such doctors existed or because they didn't have one practicing in their area.

We can't lose sight of the fact that the most important thing is for those suffering from depression to seek medical assistance, whether from a primary-care doctor, a psychologist, a psychiatrist, or a psychopharmacologist.

Chapter 7

Patients, Doctors, and Depression

"Just like other illnesses, depression can be treated so that people can live happy, active lives."
—Tom Bosley, American actor

JUST MAKING A DOCTOR'S APPOINTMENT CAN BE DIFFICULT FOR those suffering from depression, but thankfully, in my case, I knew something was wrong and that something warranted a trip to see a doctor. But I also was lucky in that my first doctor was a psychopharmacologist working as an intern for psychopharmacologist Dr. Scheftner. His experience allowed him to diagnose what I had and to help me. Under his care—and on several medications—I was out of my first depression within six months. Because the internist was leaving the area, he transferred me into Dr. Scheftner's care for any follow-up. At that point, I didn't realize that I would have more episodes of depression—I was just grateful to have gotten through the depression rather quickly and "back to normal."

I realize that not everyone suffering from depression has the luxury of sticking with the same doctor throughout their entire life, but that happened to me with Dr. Scheftner. I started going to him 38 years ago when I was 24 years old. He has seen me through my whole adult lifetime and the various depressions I've had in the interim.

With my history of depression, I learned that patients should know as much as they can about the disease and the medical professional treating them. The biggest thing for me—and the reason that I was able to persevere and understand things—is that right at the beginning, my doctor explained to me what I had. In our brains, we have chemicals that make us feel good, such as endorphins (a runner's high, for example), and others that create how we feel. When you are depressed, these synapses between brain cells are closed so the natural brain chemicals that make us feel good are not flowing properly. At that moment, the disease ceased to be a mystery and became something with a name, something that could be addressed and treated.

Here are some other factors for a patient with depression to keep in mind when choosing a doctor:

> **Type of doctor.** Although primary-care physicians and psychologists know how to treat genetic depression, they don't have the experience of a psychopharmacologist. It's best to find the most specialized doctor you can to treat your depression because it might mean a faster recovery. (See Chapter 6 for more on what each doctor can and can't do for depressed patients.)
>
> **Role.** It's the doctor's role to help a patient recover, and it's the patient's role to do what the doctor says, especially in terms of taking medications, etc. "I always tell my patients that if you're alive, I can get you better," says Dr. Scheftner. "But if you're dead, I can't do anything."

Explanations. Doctors should clarify their diagnosis and instructions, not just in clinical terms, but in a way that the patient can understand. It's invaluable to have a doctor who takes the time to explain what's happening to the brain of a depressed person, what causes the depression, and what steps are being taken to treat the disease.

Listening. Doctors should have enough time to listen attentively. Finding a doctor who will take the time to really hear what you are saying can be a crucial part of your recovery.

Assertiveness. You'll want a doctor who will prescribe an aggressive treatment when necessary because your chances of getting better are very good when that is the case, according to Dr. Scheftner. Treatment plans should be tailored to the patient, and patients who don't respond to initial therapies should receive additional interventions.

Ask your primary-care physician for a referral. Call your local teaching hospital for a list of names of doctors in the psychiatry department who treat depression. If this seems too insurmountable because of your illness, I'm sure a family member would be happy to assist you in this way.

If you are suffering from depression, having the right relationship with your medical professional is essential to your recovery. I strongly urge you to find a doctor who will be more than someone who diagnoses you, but also someone who is beside you and committed to helping you get through your journey out of depression.

Chapter 8

Families, Doctors, and Depression

"My hope is that one day, doctors would be able to run a test and know which medication would help the depressed patient. That way the patient would get better faster."
—Donna Litzsinger, my mother

Families with a member who has depression can feel pulled in many different directions. They can be as overwhelmed by the disease as the person suffering from it. What's essential is that they understand as much as possible what doctors can do to help their depressed family member—such knowledge will help the family to provide as much encouragement and support as possible.

I was very fortunate in that my family was absolutely supportive and there for me, but learning that supportive role took many years. They knew me and they knew the symptoms of depression. My father and brother eventually met with my psychopharmacologist privately to let him know that it didn't seem like the medications were working because they could see something that I couldn't during my depression. "All of Mark's siblings helped him whenever they could," says my mother. "We're a very close family and when anyone's in trouble, we all pitch in to help. In that way, Mark was very lucky to have that support."

But my family had different views about the doctor's role—and theirs. "The doctor was helpful as best he could," says my sister Robin. "However, I'm not sure he told us anything that was different from what we already knew about how we could help Mark." My brother, Todd, felt challenged in his supportive role, noting that "Mark literally didn't want us involved with his therapies—medical or general. But I kept encouraging him to let us get involved, especially in the early days before the depression developed into a major episode."

Sometimes, people with depression become very defensive. I know that's how I got even though my family was trying to help me. My family created a roadmap of options to help me through the depression. My father and Todd went over with my doctor the different things that might help me overcome the depression. They also discussed what to look for to see if I was sliding back into a depressive episode. In my final, worst depression at 47 years old, it got to the point where my father and brother had to call my medical doctor and make an appointment to talk with him without me because I wasn't improving at all.

"We sat down with the doctor and said, 'What can we do? It's gotten to the point that he can't take care of himself,'" says Todd. "We really felt that he was a danger to others because he wasn't of sound mind. And he was also jeopardizing his job because he couldn't function and do his job well."

That's the kind of advocacy you need on your side because the doctors may not be fully aware of how bad someone's depression has become. "I think sometimes when you've seen someone for so long, sometimes there is a little bit of tunnel vision, and they don't see things as we see them every day," notes Todd. "Mark probably put on a good show for the doctor. So our intervention was very important to get the doctor to realize that Mark's depression was jeopardizing Mark's long-term health."

It's also crucial to let your loved one's doctor or medical team know if the person is suicidal. More than 90 percent of those who commit suicide have been diagnosed with clinical depression or another mental disorder.[98] Risk factors include previous suicide attempts, a family history of suicide or mental disorder/substance abuse, family violence, physical or sexual abuse, and accessible firearms (see "Suicide Warning Signs" for more signs). "We're thankful that we never had a feeling of Mark feeling low in a way that he would want to off himself. I've seen that with other people, but I never felt or saw that with him," says Todd. "And for that we are grateful."

Sometimes family members can be the advocate with the doctor when depression prevents the patient from doing so. "I remember hearing this from Mark, 'Well, my doctor is adjusting this. My doctor is adjusting that,'" recalls Todd. "During this third episode, we went to talk to the doctor because we realized that the medication adjustments just weren't working. That's when he [the doctor] suggested electroconvulsive therapy." (See Chapter 12 for more about shock therapy.)

If my family hadn't seen that the medications weren't working and knew that something else needed to be tried, I might not have gotten help as soon as I did. I was very glad I had given permission for my family to talk with my doctors because of the extra support that provided me during my depression episodes.

Suicide Warning Signs[99]

If your loved one suffers from depression, there's a chance he or she might become suicidal. You should always view talk of suicide as serious. You can get help by calling 800-SUICIDE (800-784-2433), 800-273-TALK (800-273-8255), or 800-799-4889 (for the hearing impaired).

Here are the warning signs of suicide. Contact a medical professional or call the suicide hotline immediately if you suspect your loved one might be contemplating suicide.

- Constant talk or thoughts of death, including talk of suicide
- Clinical depression (deep sadness, trouble sleeping/eating, loss of interest) that worsens
- Tempting "death" by risky behavior (running red lights, driving too fast)
- Loss of interest in what used to interest the person, such as a change in hobby or activity participation
- Comments about worthlessness, helplessness, or hopelessness
- Putting affairs in order (updating wills, organizing papers, etc.)
- Saying phrases like "I want out" or "It would be better if I wasn't around"
- Drastic, sudden change from very sad to very happy or calm
- Telling people "goodbye"
- Past suicide attempts

Part III
The Treatment

Chapter 9

Depression Treatments in the Twentieth Century

"The beauty of depression, if there is one, is that the depressed person rarely remembers anything of the episode when they come out of it."
—Dick Litzsinger, my father

TREATMENTS FOR DEPRESSION CHANGED A GREAT DEAL DURING the twentieth century, progressing from the advent of psychotherapy through the invention of antidepressant medications. The last century saw myriad different approaches to treating the disease, many of which proved beneficial to patients.

At the beginning of the twentieth century, the relatively new field of psychoanalysis, which emerged in the late nineteenth century, started exploring how to treat depressed people without medication. Spearheaded by pioneering psychiatrists Sigmund Freud and Carl Jung, this process involved treating patients by listening and talking.

Around the 1950s, the invention of antidepressant medications gradually grew to become the most popular form of physical treatment for depression, replacing earlier physical treatments such as shock therapy and surgery.

It wasn't until 1980 that the disease of depression was officially classified as a condition by itself that could clearly be treated distinctly from other mental health conditions. "There was no specific disease of depression prior to the 1980 edition of the American Psychiatric Association's *Diagnostic and Statistical Manual-III (DSM-III)*—although there were disease categories of manic-depressive psychosis and individual melancholia that shared a few of the same features as the current diagnosis of depression."[100]

By the end of the twentieth century, both psychoanalysis and antidepressant medications had gained ground and became popular treatments for depressed patients. Many times, those two treatments went hand-in-hand as a part of a comprehensive plan to treat depression by improving every aspect of a person's overall health—body, mind, and spirit.

"In general medicine, the average primary-care physician used to take the attitude of avoidance when confronted with a patient with depression symptoms," says Dr. Pollack with Rush University Medical Center. "It was too difficult to help such a person. But now that has changed with the realization about opportunities to screen patients for depression and the recognition of ways to help those more easily."

A closer look at the treatments of the last century will lay the groundwork for the way depression is being treated today. Much of the work of the twentieth century guided depression treatments away from the inhumane and sometimes barbaric practices of the past toward more enlightened treatment. "Currently, we now enjoy a more nuanced view of the person that encompasses development and lifestyle issues as well as the context of how people interact with their environment," explains Dr. Pollack.

Here is a timeline of depression treatments:

1910s/1920s: A FOCUS ON ALLEVIATING SYMPTOMS

During the earliest decades of the twentieth century, most people with a mental illness diagnosis of any kind, including depression, found themselves in mental hospitals. With depression not yet classified as a distinct disease, doctors and therapists simply focused on depressed people's symptoms (such as sorrow and lethargy) with whatever treatments they thought could best alleviate those symptoms. For some, this meant physical treatment plans, such as changing their diet, getting more sleep, and following bathing or exercise regimens. For others, that meant counseling through the new field of psychoanalysis.

Most practitioners focused their study on the alleviation of symptoms at this time, in large part because disease concepts had yet to be well defined. "But though both psychiatrists and neurologists emphasized the relief of symptoms, symptom relief meant different things in different treatment settings."[101]

Generally speaking, psychiatrists favored allopathic treatments ("a system of medical practice that aims to combat disease by use of remedies [as drugs or surgery] producing effects different from or incompatible with those produced by the disease being treated"),[102] which led to creative therapies during the first half of the twentieth century. Some of those therapies had dangerous elements, such as gastric lavage (the washing out of the stomach with sterile water or a saline solution) for indigestion and constipation. Extreme methods were used to activate lethargic patients or calm agitated patients. The goal of treatment was to get the patient well enough to leave the hospital. "Although psychiatrists focused on the hospital context, neurologists in the first part of the century treated depressive symptoms in the same way as other types of symptoms, particularly with an emphasis on rest and feeding."[103]

The most common type of treatment for depressed patients during these years was psychoanalysis. In this type of therapy, the patient reclined on a couch nearly every day for an hour with the analyst out of view but in the room. While relaxing, "the patient simply allowed her mind to wander and spoke whatever thoughts came into her head, however odd, embarrassing, vexing, or socially unacceptable."[104]

The analyst would then analyze the stream of talk for patterns and inconsistencies before making suggestions to the patient as to their meaning or implications. "Through this iterative [repetitive] process of free thought, speaking aloud the thoughts, and interacting with the analyst, the patient would gradually gain access to the repressed thoughts lying in her unconscious, bring them to the realm of the conscious, and resolve the decades-old fears and anxieties with a sensible adult framework."[105]

Psychoanalysis fell out of favor for depression treatments in the latter part of the twentieth century, but doctors are now realizing the important link between mind and body, and seek to restore a person's whole being through various treatments. But a century ago, the tenuous results of psychoanalysis on depression patients paved the way for more radical methods.

1930s/1940s: DRASTIC MEASURES

A growing sense of dissatisfaction about the effectiveness of depression treatments coupled with alarm about the despair many depressed patients suffered in mental institutions led to the development of more drastic depression treatments. By the 1930s and 1940s, Americans revolted over the state of big psychiatric hospitals because of overcrowding, often horrific living conditions, and patients' overall hopeless attitudes.

These institutions promoted an assortment of extreme interventions, including psychosurgery and convulsive therapies.

The new treatments involved often highly invasive procedures, such as lobotomies (surgically destroying the frontal lobes of patients' brains), electroconvulsive therapy (applying electric shocks to patients' brains), and comas induced through insulin drugs. Patients who weren't experiencing significant healing from depression through psychoanalysis frequently would be referred for these more severe treatments.

Although shock treatments and surgery did help alleviate depression in some people, both types of treatments were controversial. "Many patients, particularly those who had suffered severe, prolonged, and crippling depression, improved dramatically [after shock treatment]."[106] Meanwhile, lobotomy surgeries—a procedure both crude and destructive—were labeled unnecessarily harsh by detractors. However, that criticism didn't stop these treatments from continuing throughout the 1930s and '40s before declining in the '50s when doctors began prescribing antidepressant medications.

Psychoanalysis continued to be a popular form of treatment for less severely depressed patients during this era, yet because of a shortage of trained psychiatrists, many people who needed treatment for their depression didn't get it. "This psychotherapeutic reality is, indeed, grotesque. Millions of people need treatment, and only a few thousands can get it—at an exorbitant price and a tremendous sacrifice of time," wrote psychiatrist Martin Gumpert in 1946.[107]

1950s: ANTIDEPRESSANT MEDICATIONS ARRIVE

Patients around the middle of the twentieth century typically sought either psychotherapy or medications to treat their depression—but not both. That was because physicians at that time thought that depression could be neatly categorized into two distinct types, each of which required a different type of treatment. "Influenced by hundreds of years of back and forth debate as to whether depression was best thought of as a mental or physical problem, and by increasing knowledge of the brain and brain chemistry, the medical community of the 1950s and '60s accepted a classification that divided depression into subtypes based on supposed causes of the disorder."[108]

Endogenous depression was thought to come from within the body and caused by a physical problem or genetics. Reactive or neurotic depression was triggered by significant environmental change, such as job loss, death of a spouse, etc. People diagnosed with endogenous depression sought physical treatments (medications), while people diagnosed with neurotic depression sought mental/emotional treatments (psychotherapy).

Then antidepressant medications arrived on the scene in the 1950s. "In 1952, doctors noticed that a tuberculosis medication (isoniazid) was also useful in treating people with depression. Shortly after this significant finding, the practice of using medications to treat mental illness gained full steam."[109] From that point on, medications became the first line of defense in mental illness treatment.

"This development corresponded with a shift in medical thinking from depression as a purely emotional issue to a brain disease fixable by medication," says Dr. Pollack. "The discovery of the antidepressant use of a TB medication helped that transition along."

The two early antidepressant drugs Imipramine and Marsilid established the foundations of how doctors understood and prescribed medications to treat depression during the late 1950s. Scientists used the action of these antidepressant drugs to draw conclusions about the nature of the illness. Both Imipramine and Marsilid worked differently, but led to the same result in the end.

Those drugs trigger larger amounts of the neurotransmitter norepinephrine to conjugate in the synapses (micro-spaces between the brain's nerve cells), which allow the brain cells to "talk" via chemical gestures. "Drugs in Impiramine's family, the tricyclics, do this by blocking the re-absorption, or reuptake, of norepinephrine from the synapse back into the nerve cells around it. Drugs in Marsilid's family, which came to be known as 'MAO inhibitors,' or MAOIs, do it by dampening the action of an enzyme that breaks down certain neurotransmitters, norepinephrine included. MAO inhibitors also boost brain levels of another neurotransmitter, serotonin. Later research confirmed that tricyclic antidepressants do so too."[110]

The field of psychotherapy grew significantly during this era, as many new types of counseling therapies emerged. Newly minted psychotherapists from a wide variety of backgrounds began to create therapy schools based on their own experimentation with different therapeutic techniques. Most of these approaches differed only slightly in techniques but a few provided innovative treatment. "One new technique emphasized cognitive processes over emotional processes, for example, and another required behavioral interventions instead of psychological interventions."[111]

"This was partly due to the heavy influence of European psychoanalytic thinking, which thankfully didn't permeate the entire United States," notes Dr. Scheftner. But the pharmaceutical discoveries also led to a more medical approach to depression.

1960s/1970s: NEW DRUGS AND PSYCHOTHERAPY

Throughout the 1960s and '70s, pharmaceutical companies developed a plethora of new medications to treat depression, and psychiatrists began to counsel depressed patients according to a treatment approach called cognitive behavioral therapy. New medications included others in the two families of antidepressants that had emerged in the 1950s (tricyclics and MAOIs) such as Nardil, Pamelor, and Elavil, as well as drugs in a new medication family called benzodiazapenes (popularly known as tranquilizers).

These tranquilizers (such as Valium and Librium) were at first presented as medications for anyone who was seeking stress relief, not as drugs especially to treat any specific disease. Tranquilizers were "originally marketed to ease the strains of corporate life for hard-driving businessmen" and then "turned into a phenomenon"[112] as people with mental illnesses began using tranquilizers to treat their symptoms. "When lithium was released for general use in the United States, it was significant because of its effectiveness for people with bipolar disorder," says Dr. Scheftner.

The popularity of tranquilizers led more people to seek treatment for depression, even when they had a mild case. "The availability of an easy fix for a common mental problem brought many new cases out of the woodwork, and demand for psychiatric services increased."[113] Because tranquilizers could be prescribed by doctors after just one appointment, many depressed people opted to take them for short-term relief of their symptoms rather than participate in ongoing psychotherapy. As Katherine Sharpe asks in *Coming of Age on Zoloft*: "Why spend long years analyzing your problems when you can pop a pill and watch them melt away?"[114]

However, these drugs had numerous side effects and it often took many weeks to find the right dosage. That's what happened to me with my first round of antidepressants. I'd tell the doctor what was going on, that I was having ruminations and obsessive-compulsive behaviors, and he'd recommend tweaks to the medications. In a normal person, you would see some lifting of your illness within two to three weeks, but in my case it might be six to eight weeks before we'd know whether a medication was effective.

The procedures in place at this time meant weeks of waiting and adjusting dosage before the patient had any change to his illness. It was based on a regimen that was proven over time. But depending on the patient, the doctors might tweak the dosage or try different combinations in the hope that a new drug might push the main drug to do what it was supposed to do. And what worked for me might not work for you and vice versa. It was a trial-and-error process.

Adding to the frustration was the fact that to switch drugs, the patient had to wait for the previous medicine to work its way out of his or her system before starting the new medication. I always likened it to drying out like an alcoholic for a week or two before starting the new medication. When I was in the drying-out period, I was probably not getting any better and I was more likely getting a little worse because I wasn't on anything.

"The shift in the '60s away from the psycho-dynamic towards increasing usage of medications to treat depression was significant," said Dr. Pollack. That change also led to more depressed people seeking alternative methods of treatment.

Not only did depressed people in the 1960s and '70s seek easier ways to treat their disease with medication, they also tried to find easier ways to treat depression through psychotherapy (counseling). "The basic concepts that underlie the cognitive theory of depression were developed during the 1960s."[115] That approach to treating depression, which is also sometimes referred to as cognitive behavioral therapy, focuses on the connections between the patient's thoughts, feelings, and actions. The goal of cognitive therapy is for patients to learn to identify and change distorted thinking patterns, inaccurate beliefs, and unhelpful behaviors.

This new, practical approach to counseling emerged as "there was considerable dissatisfaction with psychoanalytic theory and treatment."[116] Why? Because of "its length, expense, and lack of superior efficacy over the briefer forms of therapy."[117]

That dissatisfaction with psychoanalysis set the stage for shorter and less-expensive counseling sessions to treat depression. "Thus, the controversy over the effectiveness of psychodynamic psychotherapy as well as the increased demand for brief and effective treatments created a receptive environment in the 1970s for alternative approaches to depression."[118] These new, briefer treatments often involved trying to solve specific problems in depressed patients' lives to reduce their stress levels, which counselors hoped would in turn reduce the intensity of their depression.

However, during these two decades, the tide turned toward a more biological reason for depression when the first set of relatively comprehensive diagnostic criteria in psychiatry was published in the medical journal *Archives of General Psychiatry*. "The point is you went from a diagnosis that was not well-specified to one that had specific criteria to be met," explains Dr. Scheftner.

1980s: THE AGE OF PROZAC

During the 1980s, patients suffering from severe depression still took antidepressants prescribed by psychiatrists or doctors, but those with mild depression began backing away from tranquilizers. Thus, the stage was set for a new type of medication to help depressed people.

Tranquilizers "had gone out of favor ... [because] ... stories about tranquilizer addiction had begun to appear regularly in the press, and the public's love of tranquilizers started to turn into fear and ridicule. For the time being, Americans with minor mental problems were left without a go-to medication."[119]

Then in 1987, the "blockbuster drug" Prozac burst on the scene, fueling the dramatically increased popularity of antidepressant medications in the late twentieth century. "By 1987, about 1.8 percent of Americans purchased an antidepressant each year. That's not nothing, but it's hardly the explosive proliferation that would begin in the 1990s [because of Prozac]."[120]

Prozac's introduction ushered in a new biological age. Prozac became "the most commercially successful drug in the history of the pharmaceutical industry."[121] This antidepressant regulated the brain's serotonin levels and had few side effects. Previously, psychiatrists typically wrote prescriptions for antidepressants in order to supervise the often tricky dosage. Now, Prozac promised an easy "one pill a day forever" routine that enticed general practitioners and internists to pick up their pen to write prescriptions for the drug, bypassing the traditional method of referring the patient to a trained psychiatrist or counselor. During the ten years after Prozac's debut, the number of patients seeking mental health treatment from general practitioners increased twofold.[122]

In addition, depressed people who sought treatment for their disease through psychotherapy started to go to other, less-expensive counselors who promised patients quicker, easier help. This opened the door for clinical lay therapists, social workers, and other professionals to hang their shingles to help those with mental illnesses. "Some of these newer providers crassly advertised their wares with glaring boasts of 'Success in ten weeks—or your money back,' or 'obsessions and addictions—insurance accepted.'"[123]

1990s: MANAGED CARE LIMITS ACCESS

During the last decade of the twentieth century, many health insurance companies started the controversial practice of "managed care" (trying to control costs by covering treatments only from preselected doctors and only after patients obtained permission from the insurance companies to begin treatment). Managed care limited access to treatments for some depressed patients, but those who were able to obtain insurance coverage continued to choose from among many different options in psychotherapy counseling and antidepressant medications.

Unfortunately, mental health didn't fit well with managed services. "Ambiguous diagnoses and treatment regimens, combined with uncertain outcomes, left mental health at the mercy of the gatekeepers."[124] Psychotherapy, which tended to be a more expensive treatment for depression than medication, declined even more due to managed care's attempts to limit health-care costs. "Managed care effectively ended the viability of psychoanalysis as a treatment option for almost all Americans."[125]

What was worse was the tendency of managed care to pressure Americans into medication-only treatment, rather than the combination of psychotherapy and medicine. "Some patients responded by paying their therapists from their own funds, forcing them to negotiate more carefully over hourly rates and treatment durations. Therapists, in turn, learned to market their services partially on price, meaning that those who had charged less in the past were now increasingly attractive to prospective clients."[126]

The shift also led to many people thinking about depression treatment in terms of a chemical imbalance that should be corrected if possible with drugs. Basically, psychoanalysis fell out of favor, while psychopharmacology rose in prominence. "During the 1990s, psychiatrists and ordinary people alike learned to think of a wide variety of mental problems as chemical imbalances, and came to see chemical-balancing medications as the most sensible response. The shift transformed the practice of psychiatry, with analytic methods giving way to a focus on the pharmaceutical management of symptoms."[127]

Also during the 1990s, a major new class of antidepressant medications emerged: selective serotonin reuptake inhibitor (SSRI) drugs. Prozac was the first of the SSRI medications in the late 1980s; others like Paxil, Zoloft, Celexa, Luvox, and Lexapro followed in the 1990s. "'Selective' meant that unlike earlier anti-depressants, the drug targeted only serotonin, not serotonin and norepinephrine both. The selectivity was supposed to be a selling point, the idea being that a more targeted drug would cause fewer side effects."[128]

For my first depression treatments, my doctor put me on lithium and MAOIs. After starting a new medication, I went in twice a week to have my blood drawn so the doctor could check to see how much of the medication was in my bloodstream and how the medication was working.

Those older medications had many side effects, like con-stipation and dry mouth, but the one I remember the most was the craving for sweets. Many people with depression, especially women, didn't want to take those pills because they didn't want to gain weight. One time my craving for sweets was so strong, I ordered five gallons of ice cream from the local ice cream shop and went home to enjoy it over time.

Despite the popularity of antidepressants in the 1990s, many people with depression still pursued psychotherapy in one of the many available forms of counseling (from well-trained profes-sionals to lay counselors who hadn't gone through much train-ing). "The majority of patients who sought mental health-care continued to be treated with psychotherapy alone, even though multiple studies showed that most people improved faster and more thoroughly when they were treated with both medication and therapy."[129]

"The other thing that starts coming out in the beginning of the 1990s is that while we now were viewing depression as this purely biologically caused event or genetically caused event, it turns out that, in fact, early life experiences really do play a certain role in some forms of depression," says Dr. Scheftner. "So the perspective has really started to change to include a mix-ture of genetic and biology as well as early childhood events and trauma as influencing later-life experiences, emotions and disease presentations like depression."

Whether patients ended up choosing counseling or medication to treat their depression, they now had many different options within those two categories to consider. The 1990s featured a "proliferation of products and services and well-meaning educational efforts designed to help treat and prevent depression. For most commentators by the 1990s, depression was a major public health problem—and it had readily available consumer solutions, including medications and other kinds of methods to deal with unhappiness, such as 'learning vacations' to help people overcome loss or disappointment."[130]

As the twentieth century drew to a close, people suffering from depression had many different treatment options to consider. "Because it has become the accepted view that depression frequently has multiple causes, including biological, psychological and social causes, it has also become the norm that multiple professions and approaches to treatment have important roles to play in helping people overcome depression."[131]

Chapter 10

Depression Treatments in the Twenty-first Century

"There's nothing, repeat, nothing to be ashamed of when you're going through a depression. If you get help, the chances of your licking it are really good. But you have to get yourself onto a safe path."
—Mike Wallace, American television journalist

T HANKS TO RECENT SCIENTIFIC ADVANCES THAT ALLOW MORE insight into the human brain and genetic makeup, medical professionals and depression patients alike are understanding depression in new ways. New depression treatments are emerging as well, so people suffering from depression have myriad potentially useful treatments to choose from as they navigate the journey toward healing. "It is very likely that future diagnostic systems will include the use of some genetic, brain-imaging, and biological markers of illness as they are discovered and correlated with characteristic symptoms, long-term course of illness, or drug responsiveness."[132]

With the recent explosion of new biological understanding fueling new ways of thinking about depression, researchers have developed a range of innovative approaches to depression that are all based on better biological knowledge in the twenty-first century. "New theories of depression are focusing on differences in neuron density in various regions of the brain; on the effect of stress on the birth and death of brain cells; on the alteration of feedback pathways in the brain and on the role of inflammation evoked by the stress response."[133]

Additionally, depressed people have begun to treat their disease in multiple ways rather than choosing one treatment, as many did in the past. This holistic approach to depression emphasizes the power of personal choice and that there are many different "pathways to wellness" for depression patients. "Although people with depression usually have similar symptoms, everyone has a unique blend of personal history, current concerns, strengths, and preferences. Instead of a 'one-size-fits-all' approach, many people with depression, and their doctors and therapists, prefer an individualized, multifaceted plan."[134]

Here are some of the treatment options currently available or in development.

GENETIC TESTS

The first map of the human genetic code—the instruction book for human life—was a watershed moment in the twenty-first century. After Dr. Francis Collins and his team at the Human Genome Project successfully mapped all of the genes people can carry within their bodies, their accomplishment ushered in a new era of medicine. Genetic knowledge now makes it possible for researchers to look for genes that cause diseases like depression, and to develop treatments that treat diseases at the most fundamental level. Because different people carry different types of genes, new treatments for depression and other diseases that arise from genetic research can be personalized to each patient, potentially offering the maximum effectiveness for every individual.

However, the new field of genetic medicine hasn't yet progressed to the point where the specific genetic causes for depression are clearly understood. Nor are there currently any new depression treatments based on genetics that have been conclusively proven to be effective. Researchers all over the world are unraveling the biological pathways to depression, searching for clues that will help doctors and patients alike understand the causes and cures of depression. "If the genetic mechanisms [of depression] can be decoded, then new medications or other biological treatments could be designed to correct these abnormalities. Although the promise of genetic studies hasn't been realized yet, there are many good leads."[135]

What's known is that "inherited traits play a role in how antidepressants affect you. In some cases, where available, results of genetic tests (done by blood test or cheek swab) may offer clues about how your body will respond to a particular antidepressant."[136] However, no one has developed a "specific diagnostic biologic test for depression at this time."[137] There are several types of tests, such as the dexamethasone suppression test, PET, and SPECT functional brain-imaging scans, and genetic-marker tests, that can help diagnose depression. But as yet, nothing has been found to "accurately determine which patients need which forms of therapy."[138]

What researchers *can* say conclusively right now is that depression "originates in genetics and family inheritance. If one of your parents, brothers, or sisters has unipolar major depression, then you have a twenty percent chance of inheriting it yourself. If both of your parents have genes for depression, you have a 50 percent chance of getting it. However, even if no one in your family has unipolar major depression, the depressive genes can occur spontaneously on their own."[139]

For me, it was a revelation to learn that genetic depression ran in my family. My Uncle Norman, a psychiatrist who first diagnosed my depression, told me he had treated my grandfather, my grandfather's brothers, and my mother for the same disease. Not only did I have a name for this malaise, but I had company in this suffering.

As I delved deeper into my family history of depression, I discovered its origins: my grandmother's side of the Folletts. All four of her sons had depression, although it was likely they called it by a different name in the early twentieth century. I can't tell you how many people in the Follett family in general had or have depression, but I do know others in the family suffered from the disease, my mother among them in her adult years.

Finding out if family members have suffered from depression can be enormously helpful to patients for a number of reasons. First, the patient knows he or she is not alone in battling this illness. Second, the patient realizes he or she wasn't responsible for contracting the disease—it was in their genes and thus unavoidable, much like other genetic diseases. Third, the patient can seek more targeted treatments.

Although there's a lack of new treatments based on genetics, some health-care providers use information from genetic tests to evaluate the effectiveness of older treatments, such as existing antidepressant drugs. For example, Dr. Deborah Serani, an American psychologist and expert on depression, advises her own patients to take a genetic-testing panel called Cytochrome p450, because it can give their medical team valuable information to choose which antidepressants may benefit them most, as well as what the optimal dosages should be. "The results gained from getting this test can minimize dangerous adverse drug interactions, side-step side effects, and offer greater confidence taking medication. ... It will significantly reduce the time and prolonged anguish of finding symptom relief by pinpointing which antidepressant medication, and what dosages, may be treatment productive."[140]

The Cytochrome p450 genetic-testing panel can help patients considering antidepressant drugs in two key ways—by identifying what a patient's genetic metabolism is for medications, and by revealing how other medications might affect the patient and alert a doctor to a potential adverse drug reaction.

BRAIN SCANS

Brain-scan technology has improved to the point where it can be a useful tool for doctors and therapists in treatment decisions. "An explosion of research in recent years has helped us understand what happens in the major centers of brain activity when people become depressed."[141]

Brain scans have revealed that the cortex, or outer layer of the brain, is the part responsible for conscious thinking. Recent findings about the anatomy of depression reveal that the cortex "becomes *underactive* in many people with depression."[142] But the limbic areas—the ones responsible for emotions like anger, joy, sadness, and happiness—become *overactive* in many depressed people. Antidepressant medications first correct the limbic abnormalities. "Studies have found that CBT [cognitive behavioral therapy] has biological effects on the brain. CBT works first by improving functioning in the front of the cortex. Thus CBT appears to work from the 'top down,' and medication appears to work from the 'bottom up.'"[143]

Brain scans show how depression diagnosed through patient interviews affects the brain. Brain-imaging studies have demonstrated that the hippocampus—a memory-forming part of the brain—becomes injured if long periods of severe depression have been left untreated. The hippocampus actually responds to such damage by growing smaller. "Antidepressants, lithium, and the anticonvulsant Depakote appear to be protective and have been shown to cause the brain to synthesize growth factors for these neurons. In other words, it now appears that depression causes brain damage and treatment reverses this."[144]

Although brain scans can show what the brains of depressed people look like after they have already been diagnosed through medical interviews, the scans can't yet reliably help doctors diagnose depression in the first place. Right now, scientists have nothing to reliably help them find unipolar depression. "There are no tests for the reduced serotonin of other neurochemicals involved in depression, because the amounts contained in the gaps between your brain cells are too tiny."[145]

Neurofeedback, often also called EEG biofeedback or brain wave training, has been used to treat specific conditions, such as attention deficit hyperactivity disorder (ADHD) and epilepsy, but some scientific studies have found promising results in treating depression, among other conditions and diseases. Basically, "neurofeedback uses sensors to detect physical changes of the body ... [by] placing small sensors on the scalp to see changes in a person's brainwave activity."[146] The treatment generally involves two or more sessions per week and has few negative side effects.

While more research is being done to see how depression patients respond to neurofeedback training, research has determined that it's an effective intervention for children with ADHD by improving impulse control and attentiveness, decreasing hyperactivity, raising intelligence scores, and improving academic performance. Qualified neurofeedback practitioners can be found through the International Society for Neurofeedback & Research.

ELECTROCONVULSIVE THERAPY

Patients suffering from severe depression may choose the more invasive treatment of electroconvulsive therapy (ECT). This treatment was used often during the early twentieth century, but now can be done without causing as many side effects such as confusion and memory loss. The treatment involves passing electrical currents through the brain while the patient is under anesthesia. ECT usually provides immediate relief from depression, especially more severe depression that hasn't responded to other treatments. "ECT is usually used for people who don't get better with medications, can't take antidepressants for health reasons, or are at high risk of suicide."[147]

ECT has a long history of being one of "the oldest and most effective treatment for severe, life-threatening depression, and modern anesthesia has eliminated most of the complications,"[148] except severe or long-term memory complaints. In the early days of ECT, the treatment was administered without any anesthesia or muscle-relaxing drugs, leading many patients to experience fear, pain, and seizures during the procedure. However, during the twenty-first century, medical teams use anesthesia and take many precautions to guard against seizures.

Although ECT is quite effective at alleviating the symptoms of depression—it has a remission rate (a decrease or disappearance of symptoms) ranging from 55 to 86 percent[149]—it's still reserved only for the most severe cases of depression. "ECT ... is used when a very rapid response is potentially life-saving—for example, when a patient is lying in bed all day, refusing to eat or dress herself, having hallucinations or delusions of sin, guilt, or punishment, and talking of wanting to be dead."[150] (See Chapter 12 for more on ECT.)

MAGNETIC STIMULATION

A new way of stimulating the brain to try to relieve depression is through transcranial magnetic stimulation (TMS), which is also called repetitive transcranial magnetic stimulation (rTMS). TMS was approved by the FDA in 2008 as a treatment for depression that hasn't improved through traditional treatments like anti-depressant medications.

TMS sends a series of magnetic pulses targeted toward brain cells their medical team hopes to stimulate. Patients remain completely conscious during TMS treatments. The treatment generally takes place while the patient reclines in a chair with a treatment coil applied to his or her scalp. Brief magnetic pulses are sent through the coil to invigorate nerve cells in the brain that regulate mood and depression. Usually, the treatment cycle runs five times a week for up to six weeks.[151]

Some doctors view TMS as a better alternative to ECT because it doesn't use anesthesia or include the risk of seizures.[152] However, the potential of TMS as a depression treatment has yet to be fully explored. "Like any very new technique, the details of how best to use it are still being explored; placement of the magnetic coils, stimulus parameters, frequency and duration of treatment, and efficacy are still being evaluated. Generally, improved outcome occurs with greater course duration, pulse intensity, and quantity."[153]

Some experts have advocated a more cautious approach to TMS. "While rTMS has been approved by the FDA for use in treatment-resistant depression, you may want to wait for more information on rTMS."[154]

VAGUS NERVE STIMULATION

Another new depression treatment that focuses on stimulating the human brain to alleviate depression is vagus nerve stimulation (VNS). This procedure was approved by the FDA in 2005 for depression that hasn't responded to other treatments. It involves a doctor surgically inserting an electrical device similar to a pacemaker in a patient's chest, connecting it to wires, and wrapping those wires around the vagus nerve that runs through the chest and connects to the brain.

However, one major drawback is that VNS works at a snail's pace compared with both antidepressant drugs and ECT. "It is not unusual to wait three to six months or more to see some response."[155] But the procedure has proven effective for some patients. "A two-year outcome study of 59 treatment-resistant depression patients receiving VNS reported one- and two-year response rates of 44 percent and 42 percent; impressively, 81 percent of patients were still receiving VNS at two years."[156]

VNS has been a useful tool for relieving depression in some patients who have suffered severe forms of the disease, but the risky procedure should be carefully considered before trying. "Despite its potential usefulness, VNS has many safety issues and is currently a rather drastic procedure for the treatment of unipolar major depression. Surgically opening your chest is a serious procedure that leaves you vulnerable to infection, and we do not yet know enough about the long-term effects of VNS on your vagus nerve or your health in general."[157]

ANTIDEPRESSANT MEDICATIONS

The main classes of medications invented in the twentieth century—tricyclics, MAOIs, and SSRIs—are still in common use today. Today, SSRIs are the most commonly prescribed of all the antidepressant medications. The medical profession often starts with an SSRI prescription because those "medications are safer and generally cause fewer side effects than other types of antidepressants. SSRIs include fluoxetine (Prozac), paroxetine (Paxil, Pexeva), sertraline (Zoloft), citalopram (Celexa), and escitalopram (Lexapro)."[158]

SSRIs in general lower aggression, anxiety, and depression, while upping appetite and weight gain. Also, these medications can have a detrimental impact on a patient's sex drive. "Serotonin antidepressants usually prolong the time to reach orgasm. Most modern antidepressants have a strong serotonin effect. Norepinephrine generally increases physical energy, motivation, and anxiety, while decreasing appetite, weight, and sleep. Dopamine tends to increase alertness, concentration, and optimism, while decreasing appetite."[159]

People who use antidepressants usually experience some success if they stick with their treatment plans, but there is still the persistent problem of some patients stopping antidepressant treatments prematurely. The key to successfully using antidepressant medications is having the right attitude about the treatment plan.

The patient's attitude toward medication during the first weeks of treatment is of paramount importance. If family members, patients, and doctors all agree that drugs are a necessary part of treatment, the chance of success is high. But if the patient or those in his support group view antidepressants as a crutch, a weakness, or unnatural, chances of long-term recovery diminish. "Similarly, if the therapist views medication as a powerful partner to psychotherapy, this attitude will strengthen the treatment plan, whereas the belief that beginning medication means the therapy is failing can be harmful."[160]

In June 2017, the U.S. Army announced it had commissioned a study on whether injecting an anesthetic into the neck would alleviate symptoms of posttraumatic stress disorder (PTSD), which soldiers often experience along with depression. "The $2 million Army study constitutes the first large-scale randomized control research into the use of shots—called stellate ganglion blocks—to treat PTSD. The injections have been used for decades for arm pain and shingles."[161] Doctors in favor of the treatment emphasize that the shots don't cure the disorder but merely "eases enough to allow talk therapy, pharmaceuticals and other approaches to achieve long-term improvements."[162]

ANTIDEPRESSANTS AND PLACEBOS

A headline-making 2008 research study (called "Initial Severity and Antidepressant Benefits: A Meta-Analysis of Data Submitted to the Food and Drug Administration") showed that placebos were just as effective against depression as antidepressant medications taken by patients in the study. The American, British, and Canadian doctors who conducted the study evaluated the placebo pills' effectiveness against that of all types of antidepressant drugs, such as tricyclics, MAOIs, and SSRIs.

The analysis conducted by the researchers of both the published and unpublished data from drug companies found that most of the benefits from antidepressants could be attributed to the placebo effect. The study's lead researcher, Dr. Irving Kirsch, explained in an article he wrote called "Antidepressants and the Placebo Effect" for the German medical psychology journal *Zeitschrift fur Psychologie* that "some antidepressants increase serotonin levels, some decrease it, and some have no effect at all on serotonin. Nevertheless, they all show the same therapeutic benefit. Even the small statistical difference between antidepressants and placebos may be an enhanced placebo effect, due to the fact that most patients and doctors in clinical trials successfully break blind."[163]

Kirsch described antidepressant medications as "the riskiest and most harmful"[164] of all possible depression treatments, stating, "If they are to be used at all, it should be as a last resort, when depression is extremely severe and all other treatment alternatives have been tried and failed."[165] (See Chapters 13, 14, and 15 for more information on different treatment options.)

COMBINING ANTIDEPRESSANTS AND THERAPY

Today more depressed people are opting for a combination of medication and psychotherapy rather than choosing one over the other. Research shows that combining the two treatment options is a smart choice in the twenty-first century.

"Psychotherapists have long argued with psychopharmacologists that depressive symptoms motivate introspection, self-awareness, struggle, growth, and change. Psychopharmacologists have argued that relief of human suffering through the use of medications is worthwhile and sometimes even life-saving. Fortunately, the psychotherapists and psychopharmacologists are gradually declaring a truce in this turf war, recognizing that collaboration and use of all appropriate treatment modalities allows the best treatment of both mind and brain."[166]

The scientific evidence proves that using both treatments can boost success. "More than thirty years of studies on medication and psychotherapy for depression have found that combining the two treatments can provide a greater overall treatment benefit than receiving medication or psychotherapy alone."[167]

PSYCHOTHERAPY

Psychotherapy in the twenty-first century offers more treatment options for depressed people. Although some people still seek therapy from medical doctors (psychiatrists), many pursue therapy through less-expensive practitioners, such as psychologists, licensed clinical social workers, clergy, lay counselors, and support groups.

According to the Mayo Clinic, two current types of therapy—cognitive behavioral therapy and interpersonal therapy—are especially effective for treating depression. Cognitive behavioral therapy helps depressed people understand how they are thinking and behaving in unhealthy ways, and helps them change those thoughts and behaviors to healthier ones. Interpersonal therapy helps patients study the significant relationships in their lives, then improve communication and learn from those relationships to alleviate their depression.

Here are some other types of therapy available for depressed people seeking help:

- **Psychoeducation (PE)** teaches patients about unipolar major depression, including the causes of it and how to alleviate the depression. Numerous studies have shown that PE has a good track record as a psychotherapy that relieves depression.[168]
- **Psychodynamic psychotherapy (PP)** has its roots in Jungian and Freudian psychoanalysis that assists the patient with learning about his or her inner self as a tool to treat depression. Although a slow process, PP has the potential to provide patients with lasting recovery from unipolar major depression. "Modern psychodynamic psychotherapy uses the interaction between psychotherapist and client as a tool to reveal internal assumptions and fantasies."[169]
- **Supportive therapy (ST)** has as its goal encouragement, reassurance, and nurturance through positive social feedback. ST reassures the patient that things are not as bad as he or she thinks and that success is right around the corner. "Unfortunately, from the depths of depression, this rosy view is often annoying ... ST can make you feel good for a while, but it might not help you make the changes that you need in your life."[170]

STRESS MANAGEMENT

The newest approaches to understanding and treating depression also emphasize the importance of managing stress. Depression genes make the brain overreact to stress, which can cascade into a domino effect. This is how it happens: when stressed, each of us secretes steroid stress hormones and excitatory neurochemicals in our brains, but those with unipolar major depression can't shut off the secretion after the stressful period ends.

Stress chemicals on high alert for long periods of time can damage and kill brain cells, which can trigger a unipolar major depression. "Moreover, after an episode of unipolar major depression begins, it also provokes the secretion of stress steroid hormones and excitatory neurochemicals. Thus, depression causes a stress reaction that builds on itself."[171]

This new focus on the role that stress plays in depression means that "depression treatments on the horizon include … long-term cognitive behavioral therapy for stress management,"[172] as well as "anti-inflammatory drugs"[173] to reduce inflammation in people's brains and elsewhere in their bodies. (See Chapter 15 on how exercise can help with stress relief in depression patients.)

DIGITAL THERAPY

A growing number of health providers have begun using digital therapy, such as web-based courses and mobile apps, to help those who suffer from depression. "Research … suggests that digital therapies augmented by coaches who are available by text or phone can be as effective as evidence-based traditional therapy in treating some people with depression."[174]

In the early 2000s, clinical psychologists started putting digital interventions for depression online. But those first efforts have evolved from essentially PowerPoint presentations to more interactive and personalized mobile apps, such as Lantern, Ginger.io, and Joyable. "They typically ask users to enter information about their moods and behaviors, then offer problem-solving suggestions, prompts to help patients retrain responses from negative situations, and daily health tips."[175]

Dr. Stephen Schueller, an assistant professor of preventive medicine at Northwestern University, views digital therapies as continuing to evolve into a more effective depression treatment option. "The future is trying to better understand how to make these apps and sites engaging," he says.[176]

However, one of the biggest hurdles in getting more depressed patients to even try one of these digital therapy options is knowing which one to trust. The PsyberGuide website headed by Schueller gives users a standardized rating system to assist in selecting products or apps for a variety of mental health concerns.

During the first part of the twenty-first century, doctors and scientists have gained fresh insight into how depression works and how new therapies and treatments combat the disease. With continued advancements in this area, patients with depression no longer have to fear the illness, but can face it with more confidence that relief can be attained.

Stress-Reduction Techniques

Here are some examples of stress-reduction techniques that depressed people may find beneficial:

- Acupuncture
- Relaxation techniques, such as yoga or tai chi
- Meditation
- Guided imagery
- Massage therapy
- Music or art therapy
- Spirituality
- Aerobic exercise

Experts advise patients not to rely solely on these therapies to treat depression, but to use such stress-management techniques alongside medication and psychotherapy.[177]

Chapter 11

Depression Treatments of the Future

"Depression is like a bruise that never goes away. A bruise in your mind. You just got to be careful not to touch it where it hurts. It's always there though."

–Jeffrey Eugenides, American novelist and short story writer

For many years, people suffering from depression have tried to find relief through two main options: counseling therapy and antidepressant medications. Counselors and doctors have tried to make educated guesses about which of the many types of therapy and/or drugs would effectively treat each of their patients. Yet despite all of that effort, many depressed people still don't find the help they need. "About 30 percent of all people with depression don't respond adequately to the available treatments. ... That's a dismal failure rate."[178]

There hasn't been much change in depression treatment choices for the past four decades, since new antidepressants such as Prozac made a big splash in the 1980s among patients looking for easier ways to fight the disease. But today, several promising new depression treatments are on the horizon. These newcomers—mental health apps for counseling, the ketamine hydrochloride drug, gene therapy, different drugs, and holistic medicine—have arisen as researchers start to think about treating depression in a more refined way. "Scientists are gaining a more nuanced picture of what depression is—not a monolithic disease, but probably dozens of distinct maladies—and they're getting closer to learning what works for which kind of ailment."[179]

MENTAL HEALTH APPS

Technology is becoming a counselor of sorts for depression patients through a variety of new mental health applications (apps) on computers and mobile devices like smartphones. These apps make counseling accessible anytime and anywhere—no appointment needed. They also reduce the embarrassment that depressed people can feel about their struggles by offering anonymity. These factors make mental health apps attractive options to those who are dealing with depression. So such apps are becoming more widespread with a plethora of apps that claim to treat depression exploding into the technology market.

However, mental health apps aren't yet regulated by the U.S. Food and Drug Administration (FDA) like depressed treatment medications, and they're too new to have had their claims verified by medical research studies. People who use them have to try them out through trial and error to discover which apps—if any—actually help them fight depression. The *Journal of Medical Internet Research* reviewed mental health apps, finding that "MHapps [mental health apps] and other technology-based solutions have the potential to play an important part in the future of mental health-care; however, there is no single guide for the development of evidence-based MHapps."[180]

So far, these apps are selling well. A market report published by MarketsandMarkets in 2016 predicted that the cognitive assessment and training market—which includes mental health apps—could be worth more than eight billion dollars by 2021.[181]

For depressed people, using a mental health app can be much easier than visiting a counselor or doctor because it can be difficult and exhausting to seek help in traditional ways. The popularity of apps "doesn't come as a surprise to mental health experts, who said the majority of people who could benefit from mental health services don't access them because of cost, lack of availability, or fear of the stigma still associated with mental illness. Even those who have health insurance can have a challenging time getting help."[182]

Mental health apps "have the potential to play an important part in the future of mental health-care, making mental health support more accessible and reducing barriers to help seeking. ... Innovative solutions to self-management of mental health issues are particularly valuable, given that only a small fraction of people suffering from mood or anxiety problems seek professional help. Even when people are aware of their problems and are open to seeking help, support is not always easily accessible, geographically, financially, or socially."[183]

Many of the mental health apps that people use today to treat depression allow users to access information and answer questions by themselves. Other apps connect them with people who try to help if possible, such as Crisis Text Hotline (which lets depressed people text with trained volunteers about their problems), Woebot (which is delivered over Facebook Messenger and "sends users a message each day to check in with them, asks them about their mood and energy levels, and draws from cognitive behavior therapy to combat self-defeating thinking"[184]), and Huddle (where people chat via video online to share their concerns with each other).

How can depressed people find reliable apps to treat the disease? Right now, the process involves simply trying some and seeing what happens as a result. *The Journal of Medical Internet Research* pointed out that mental health app developers aren't conducting thorough clinical trials to show evidence that their apps actually work, either. "MHapp developers rarely conduct or publish trial-based experimental validation of their apps. ... For a mental health intervention to be effective, there must be a process of rigorous experimental testing to guide development. Appropriate theories of engagement and implementation should also be consulted when introducing an evidence-based intervention to the public."[185]

In the current Wild West environment of mental health apps, patients may discover something that treats their depression effectively—but they may also find danger. For instance, as Techcrunch.com pointed out about one popular app: "Huddle is meant as a safe space where anyone can post their inner thoughts and talk about what's bothering them. It's not meant as a professional treatment platform. But with zero professionals, or even volunteers with some training, people could easily give bad or even dangerous advice to someone in a fragile state. Of course, there's also the inevitable cyber troll sure to pop up as the platform grows."[186]

Depressed people can search online reviews of mental health apps to help them select certain ones to try. Healthline.com reviews apps "based on their quality, user reviews, and overall reliability as a source of support for people living with depression."[187] But Healthline.com also cautioned: "These apps aren't designed to take the place of your medical care, but rather to be used in conjunction with any treatment you get."[188]

KETAMINE

Since the 1960s, ketamine has been an emergency-room staple for helping to ease the pain of children brought in with dislocated

shoulders and broken bones. Because of its fast-numbing properties, burn centers and veterinarians also use the drug, and it is also
a popular party drug dubbed "Special K." "Since 2006, dozens of
studies have reported that it can also reverse the kind of severe
depression that traditional antidepressants often don't touch."[189]
Not only is ketamine drawing attention for its results in patients
with treatment-resistant depression, but it is also capturing interest in health-care circles for its apparent ability to work much
faster than traditional antidepressants.

That breakthrough is pushing the American Psychiatric Association toward a tacit endorsement of ketamine for treatment-
resistant depression. "Experts are calling it the most significant
advance in mental health in more than half a century. They point
to studies showing ketamine not only produces a rapid and ro-
bust antidepressant effect; it also puts a quick end to suicidal
thinking."[190]

The U.S. Food and Drug Administration (FDA) hasn't yet
approved ketamine for use as an antidepressant, but anesthesiolo-
gists have been using ketamine since 1970 in large doses to put
people to sleep before surgery, and clinical studies on using it to
treat depression are eliciting excitement from both doctors and
patients. "'It's been a paradigm shift, that now we can achieve
rapid antidepressant effects,' says Dr. Carlos Zarate, chief of
the experimental therapeutics and pathophysiology branch at the
National Institute of Mental Health and one of the foremost researchers of ketamine. 'Now we know there's something radically
different.'"[191]

As evidence mounts of ketamine's effectiveness in treating
depression, full FDA approval for it to be prescribed freely as an
antidepressant may be coming soon. The achievement of ketamine in helping previously untreatable depressed patients get
better has an increasing number of academic medical centers,
including the Cleveland Clinic, the Mayo Clinic, the University

of California at San Diego, and Yale University, prescribing ketamine for severe depression. One San Francisco psychiatrist dubbed ketamine "the next big thing," noting the long-term success rate of many of her own patients.

A recent Rolling Stone.com article about ketamine described the fast track that ketamine seems to be on: "The FDA has yet to give ketamine the green light for treatment as an antidepressant, which means anyone using the substance is doing it off-label and footing the bill. ... The FDA granted intranasal esketamine a breakthrough therapy designation twice in the last four years—first in November 2013 for treatment-resistant depression, then again in August 2016 for severe depression with imminent risk of suicide. The designation helps speed up development of the ketamine-based drug, which is undergoing a phase III trial. ... According to the National Institutes of Health, more than ninety clinical trials studying ketamine's antidepressant properties are either underway or have completed."[192]

However, the U.S. Food and Drug Administration (FDA) has not approved ketamine for use in treating depression—the only approved usage is as an anesthetic. At least one drug company, Janssen Pharmaceutica, is conducting tests on esketamine, a nasal spray form that could be used to treat depression. Janssen indicated plans to submit the nasal spray to the agency for approval by 2019.[193] The agency has, however, "designated esketamine a 'break-through therapy,' which means it can speed through the typically lengthy drug development process and get to market more quickly. If the ongoing efficacy trials prove successful, Janssen could file esketamine for FDA approval in 2018."[194]

Exactly how ketamine works to treat depression is still unclear, but researchers think they have some idea of the process involved. Studies have found that ketamine can reduce functional connectivity of the subgenual anterior cingulate cortex, a collar-like region near the front of the brain that's connected to the prefrontal and frontal cortexes. The unique position of the anterior cingulate cortex allows it to control emotion, impulse control, decision making, and reward anticipation. Research suggests ketamine decreases "the 'over-wiredness' of the emotional regulation area. … In other words: Severely depressed people on ketamine may feel relief from repetitive thoughts of worthlessness and inadequacy."[195]

A WebMD.com article on ketamine noted that "in a handful of ketamine clinics around the country, people who weren't helped by standard treatments are getting a series of infusions to ease their depression. The drug has also been used in emergency rooms for curbing suicidal thoughts, making it a potential lifesaver. … Ketamine acts quickly—often within hours or less—and health-care professionals who give it to patients at therapeutic doses say it has mild and brief side effects in most people. But it hasn't been thoroughly studied for long-term safety and effectiveness."[196]

While ketamine shows exciting promise as a depression treatment, doctors caution that depression patients shouldn't view ketamine as a magic solution to all of their depression problems. Psychiatrist Dr. Alan Manevitz said in the WebMD.com article that "ketamine is not a miracle drug at all. It may momentarily take them away from that catastrophic place they're in with depression, but you're not addressing the rest of the patient. It's a complex issue to treat psychiatric issues, and you have to treat the whole patient."[197]

Ketamine can be addictive, so that's another issue that patients have to keep in mind. More research can help determine the optimal doses for treating depression without causing addiction. "The positive results so far don't mean a person with severe depression should use ketamine as a treatment tool outside of a clinical setting. Ketamine has addictive properties, so there is some risk for long-term substance abuse."[198]

Time will tell how well ketamine will help depression patients in the future. "Earlier this year, the APA [American Psychological Association] task force released a consensus statement in *JAMA Psychiatry* that acknowledged ketamine's effects on depression and other mood disorders, but also noted its limited data concerning its effectiveness and safety. ... It's potentially one of the most interesting new treatments to be developed in the treatment of depression in decades and it holds great promise, ... But we have to keep our eyes open to the potential risk and the fact that we still really aren't sure how to use this drug in the long-term."[199]

GENE THERAPY

Another depression treatment that looks promising for the future is gene therapy. Now in the experimental stage, gene therapy pinpoints specific genes that contribute to depression in individual patients and aims to change those genes in ways that relieve depression in those patients. (See the genetic tests section on page 82 for more on hereditary depression.)

Many people with depression could have maladaptive genes that affect arousal, hormone levels, neural activation, neurotransmission, and personality development. "In the future, it is thought that gene therapy could allow medical professionals to treat depression via modification (insertion) of a specific gene. In theory, this would target maladaptive genes that contribute to depression, and correct them via insertion of the more favorable genes. The technique of gene therapy uses a vector (most often viral) to transport a gene to specific cells where the gene is required. After the gene has been successfully inserted, the gene is processed by the cells, and proteins are manufactured. The manufactured proteins then follow specific orders (as dictated by their programming) within cells."[200]

In 2016, a major breakthrough in researching gene therapy to treat depression happened. A research study of nearly 460,000 people (conducted by scientists from Massachusetts General Hospital, Pfizer Pharmaceuticals, and the commercial genetic testing company 23andMe) revealed "no fewer than fifteen discrete regions on the human genome associated with the development of major depressive disorder (MDD). ... If depression is a breakdown in the operating system that is the human brain, the new study may have pinpointed the bad lines of code responsible."[201] Investigators for the large study used genetic information from some people who had seen a doctor for symptoms of depression, but they also used data from other people who had never done so.

What the researchers will do with this new data is unclear at this time. "In the short term, it might be possible to use the new information to refine the existing way depression is treated— developing more finely targeted drugs to adjust neurotransmitters in more precisely targeted ways, say. But the more ambitious goal is to try to stop depression before it even gets to the point that it needs to be treated. That could mean identifying at-risk people long before the onset of the disease and pharmaceutically targeting the proteins that the anomalous genes produce."[202]

One of the study's authors, Dr. Roy Perlis, director of the Center for Experimental Drugs and Diagnostics at Massachusetts General Hospital, says that identifying the 15 genetic regions that are linked to depression can pave the way for the development of new, personalized medicine treatments for the disease. "Understanding what these depression genes do in the body makes it easier for scientists to find new drugs and interventions that have the opposite effect, which will make the search for treatments ever more precise. 'It essentially gives us a target to aim at,' Perlis says."[203]

Gene therapy is proving to be effective on rodents, and when it comes time to try it out on human beings, many new depression treatments might be possible. "There are a variety of therapeutic targets to be considered in depression. Many of these genetic biomarkers already have been documented as targets for novel antidepressant drugs. That said, if we look into the future, gene therapy may prove more effective with less side effects than pharmaceuticals. The most obvious therapeutic target for depression is that of p11. Low levels of p11 expression within the nucleus accumbens is associated with depressive behavior in rodents. Further, low levels of p11 have been confirmed in the brains of humans with depression—making it a logical first target for gene therapy. ... While gene therapy hasn't yet been studied in humans for the treatment of depression, preliminary rodent studies highlight its efficacy."[204]

FUTURE MEDICATIONS

Lately, medical researchers have been dabbling with using medication to treat depression in different ways than in the past. For example, scientists in the United Kingdom believe that "depression could be treated using anti-inflammatory drugs ... after determining that it is a physical illness caused by a faulty immune system."[205]

In 2016, the National HS filled more than 64 million antidepressant prescriptions, a two-fold increase in ten years. "Current treatment is largely centered around restoring mood-boosting chemicals in the brain, such as serotonin, but experts now think an overactive immune system triggers inflammation throughout the entire body, sparking feelings of hopelessness, unhappiness, and fatigue."[206]

Recent papers and clinical trials have supported the finding that by treating inflammation, depressive symptoms abate. "The immune system triggers an inflammatory response when it feels it is under threat, sparking wide-ranging changes in the body such as increasing red blood cells, in anticipation that it may need to heal a wound soon. ... But recent studies have shown that nerve cells in the brain are linked to immune function and one can have an impact on the other."[207]

As professor Sir Robert Lechler, president of the Academy of Medical Sciences, says, "You can't separate the mind from the body. ... The immune system does produce behavior. You're not just a little bit miserable if you've got a long-term condition, there is a real mechanistic connection between the mind, the nervous system, and the immune system."[208] This connection might lead to a new field that would study the connection (synonym) between the immune system and neurology.

Another interesting breakthrough related to medication is the idea of those at risk for depression to take a preventive pill to ward off the disease. This particular idea (synonym) came about as a result of medical professionals trying to head off depression in head and neck cancer patients, who are known to be vulnerable to developing depression while undergoing cancer treatment. A group of researchers looked at "what would happen if non-depressed patients were given antidepressants before receiving treatment for head and neck cancer. ... Patients taking an antidepressant were 60 percent less likely to experience depression compared with peers who were given a placebo."[209]

This prophylaxis (preventive) approach has shown promise with other high-risk patients as well, including those suffering from hepatitis C, strokes, and melanoma. "These findings provide compelling reasons for physicians and patients to consider using these medicines to preempt mental-health issues."[210] But the prophylaxis approach has its drawbacks, especially relating to the lack of guidelines for how to implement this treatment. It's also "not clear how long patients should stay on these medications or at what level of risk someone warrants prophylaxis antidepressants."[211]

Another consideration is how the patient would handle the side effects of antidepressants, which could impact the other medical treatments as well. In addition, critics have wondered "about the financial incentives behind those who are promoting prophylactic antidepressants," given that at least one study had the lead author on the payroll of a pharmaceutical company that manufactured the antidepressant used.[212]

Finally, adding another patient population that takes antidepressants would significantly enlarge the number of Americans on such medications. "Expanding the use of antidepressants to people who have never had depression could substantially increase national consumption of psychiatric medications."[213] However, these recent studies do suggest that "doctors may be able to prepare patients for challenging situations in ways that protect them from sliding into clinical depression. Some patients may benefit from early use of antidepressants, others with therapy or a combination of the two."[214]

MICROBES AND DEPRESSION

Can bacteria in our guts help in the fight against depression? In some cases, the answer appears to be yes. Although "the notion that the state of our gut governs our state of mind dates back more than 100 years,"[215] it's only been recently that scientists have revisited that correlation. Today, gut bacteria has become the unlikely hero in our quest for better health, with probiotics being added to numerous foods, such as yogurts, and holistic practitioners touting the healing properties of microbes.

In recent years, researchers have begun studying the relationship between gut bacteria and depression, finding "tantalizing hints about how the bacteria in the gut can alter the way the brain works."[216] Preliminary research on lab mice have shown that having "the right bacteria in your gut could brighten mood and perhaps even combat pernicious mental disorders including anxiety and depression."[217]

The gut-brain connection appears to go both ways—"the brain acts on gastrointestinal and immune functions that help to shape the gut's microbial makeup, and gut microbes make neuro-active compounds, including neurotransmitters and metabolites that also act on the brain."[218] In studies conducted on mice, researchers found interesting relationships between good gut bacteria and good mental health. One Japanese study from ten years ago "showed for the first time that intestinal microbes could influence stress responses in the brain and hinted at the possibility of using probiotic treatments to affect brain function in beneficial ways."[219] Other research appears to confirm that "our guts play a role in our emotions and perhaps even our behavior."[220]

It's early days in gut-brain research, "but so far, the results are compelling. … [scientists] are amassing evidence that they hope will lead to 'psychobiotics'—bacteria-based drugs made out of live organisms that could improve mental health."[221] In the meantime, to maintain a healthy gut, eat fermented foods (kefir, kimchi, kombucha, miso, and yogurt) to give your gut bacteria diversity; avoid processed foods and food additives as much as possible, especially artificial sweeteners, which can alter metabolism; lower your overall stress level; and consume more plants.[222]

HOLISTIC MEDICINE

While people have been using holistic treatments to battle depression for a long time, the spotlight is now on several kinds of holistic treatments that are becoming increasingly popular. These treatments go beyond the traditional ways of treating depression holistically—eating a nutritious diet and getting enough sleep and exercise—to acting as natural medicines that may replace traditional antidepressants for some patients. "So-called natural remedies for depression aren't a replacement for medical diagnosis and treatment. However, for some people certain herbal and dietary supplements do seem to work well, … but more studies are needed to determine which are most likely to help and what side effects they might cause."[223]

"Typically, mental health conditions are looked at as separate from the rest of the body," says Suzanne Norman,[224] a holistic health practitioner in Libertyville, Illinois. "The holistic approach protocol employs diet and stress management along with mind and body practices to address the depressive symptoms."[225] Sometimes, holistic medicines are used along with those practices. Three holistic medicines that have gotten a lot of attention as depression treatments of the future are St. John's wort, SAMe (S-adenosylmethionine), and omega-3 fatty acids. All of them "show promise" for relieving depression.

St. John's wort is an herbal supplement that has yet to receive the FDA's stamp of approval in the United States, but in Europe, it's been a popular treatment for depression.[226] Some recent research shows why "St. John's wort is actually one of the most effective herbal remedies to try for depression."[227] Research studies number in the dozens on the way this herb helps those with depression. "'Overall, we found that the St. John's wort extracts tested in the trials were superior to placebos and as effective as standard antidepressants, with fewer side effects.' In other words, it works."[228]

SAMe, a supplement that's a synthetic form of a chemical occurring naturally in the human body, isn't yet approved by the FDA as an official depression treatment in the United States, but is widely prescribed by doctors to treat depression in Europe— just like St. John's wort.[229] The Mayo Clinic cautions that SAMe needs more studies to prove its efficacy, but the chemical appears to be effective in the short term.[230]

Omega-3 fatty acids are healthy fats that are found in foods like fish and nuts. Nutritional supplements of omega-3 fatty acids are becoming popular as depression treatments. "Omega-3 fatty acids such as eicosapentaeoic acid (EPA) and docosahexaenoic acid (DHA) might have an impact on depression because these compounds are widespread in the brain. ... The evidence is not fully conclusive, but omega-3 supplements are an option. One to two grams of omega-3 fatty acids daily is the generally accepted dose for healthy individuals, but for patients with mental disorders, up to three grams has been shown to be safe and effective."[231] The Mayo Clinic noted that "although eating foods with omega-3 fatty acids appears to have heart-healthy benefits, more research is needed to determine if it has an effect on preventing or improving depression."[232]

While these holistic medicines seem promising as depression treatments of the future, patients should carefully consider if using them is wise. Nutritional supplements such as St. John's wort, SAMe, and omega-3 fatty acids are not currently regulated by the FDA in the United States, so "you can't always be certain of what you're getting and whether it's safe. It's best to do some research before starting any dietary supplement."[233]

It's also important for people with depression to inform their doctors about any supplements they've decided to take. Both St. John's wort and SAMe have been shown to interfere with some prescription antidepressant medications, so depression patients shouldn't take them together.[234] Before trying to treat depression through supplements, people should find out how those supplements can affect other medicines they're taking.

Holistic medicine also encompasses non-supplemental treatments. Norman points out that she works with patients diagnosed with depression on "balancing their stressors in life. A big part of my job is getting people reconnected with their bodies because every choice they make can impact that balance."

For example, she specifically addresses chronic pain, emotional imbalances or periods of emotional pain, physical well-being, body nourishment, and stress levels.

Holistic protocols now being rediscovered by medical professionals like Norman have been used for thousands of years. "To bring them into our contemporary medicine models demystifies these holistic ways that allows more people to receive the benefits from this approach," she says. More scientific studies are looking into how effective holistic medicine is in treating a variety of diseases, including depression. "It's a slow process in some parts of the United States, but more studies are coming out in support of holistic medicine, and the public perception that this is a viable alternative to treatment for diseases like depression is growing," Norman says.

Each day, we learn more about depression and how it affects the patient, along with new ways to treat the symptoms and the disease itself. These newer possibilities bring hope to those suffering from depression for whom traditional treatments aren't working.

Chapter 12

Electroconvulsive Therapy Treatment and Depression

"Mark's electroconvulsive therapy treatments were the best thing in the world for him. While he didn't show improvement immediately, as he continued the course of the treatments, he gradually moved out of the deep depression."

—Robin Litzsinger, my sister

SHOCK TREATMENT, OR ECT, HAS BEEN A HIGHLY CONTROVERSIAL form of treatment for depression ever since it was first developed in 1938. It involves sending an electrical current through a patient's brain that is powerful enough to cause a convulsion similar to an epileptic seizure. In the process, the brain's chemistry undergoes changes that relieve the patient's depression. Because of the success rate of shock treatment for people suffering from the most severe cases of depression, doctors continue to proscribe its use today. "The modern version of ECT, far from outmoded, is the most effective therapy available for severe, treatment-resistant depression and bipolar disorder (and even sometimes, when deployed early enough, schizophrenia)."[235]

In part, the controversy and fear surrounding ECT has been fueled by its depiction on the silver screen in movies such as *The Snake Pit* (1948), *One Flew Over the Cuckoo's Nest* (1975), *Frances* (1982), and *Shine* (1996). Some patients who underwent shock treatment in these movies—and in real-life examples of early ECT—experienced significant side effects such as confusion, memory loss, heart problems, and broken bones. "There is no treatment in psychiatry more frightening than electroconvulsive therapy. ... There is also no treatment in psychiatry more effective than ECT."[236]

During the early years of its history, shock treatment was administered with little regard for the patient's well-being. For example, ECT was often given to patients without anesthesia; patients today are anesthetized to prevent them from injuring themselves during muscle spasms caused by seizures. Also, doctors or medical staff didn't carefully monitor shock treatments to ensure electrical dosages were precise and didn't check patients' vital signs frequently during the procedure.

Those oversights meant ECT posed a greater risk to patients in the past than it does today. However, the memory of these risks and side effects contribute to the controversy surrounding shock therapy as a depression treatment today, with better results from more targeted procedures. "A procedure pioneered in the 1930s that seemed on the verge of extinction just a generation ago is being performed today at medical centers large and small. ... Madness no more, electric shock is quietly being resurrected as a restorative wonder that someday could rank right up there with penicillin and Prozac. ... How one of the most reviled psychiatric procedures is fast becoming one of its mainstays is ... a narrative that begins with an epidemic of mental illness that has stubbornly resisted a cure, and a handful of doctors who have equally stubbornly refused to give up on a remedy that most had banished as barbaric."[237]

A VIABLE OPTION FOR SEVERE CASES OF DEPRESSION

Patients usually pursue ECT only when they suffer from severe depression and haven't found enough relief from other forms of treatment. In particular, two types of patients tend to use shock therapy to treat their depression: suicidal patients, and pregnant women who want to avoid the risks sometimes associated with antidepressants. "People who are afraid of taking their lives may request convulsant therapy as the only treatment that can stop their depression and suicidality right away. Also, pregnant women who are so severely depressed that they are endangering their own lives and the lives of their babies can request convulsant therapy to put a rapid end to their depression. Most authorities agree that convulsant therapy is safer than medications for the baby because the convulsive stimulation bypasses the unborn child."[238]

Nowadays, ECT is used to treat severe depression for patients suffering from psychosis (detachment from reality), suicidal thoughts, not eating, and depression that doesn't respond to other treatments. "ECT may be a good treatment option when medications aren't tolerated or other forms of therapy haven't worked. In some cases, ECT is used during pregnancy, when medications can't be taken because they might harm the developing fetus, in older adults who can't tolerate drug side effects, in people who prefer ECT treatments over taking medications, [and] when ECT has been successful in the past."[239]

THE EARLY YEARS OF SHOCK THERAPY

ECT emerged as a treatment for depression in 1938 and went on to become widely used to treat severe cases of depression in the mid-twentieth century—despite the fact that it was associated with serious risks at that time. "Long ago, doctors witnessed immediate and dramatic depression recoveries after their patients had seizures, and they conceived of the seizure as a treatment [for depression]."[240] That discovery led to the development of shock therapy.

"Historically, there has been a long association of seizures and general improvement in psychiatric patients," says Dr. Scheftner. "For example, patients who have partial complex seizures often become irritable and unsociable prior to a seizure. After they have a seizure, they return to their usual personalities."

Early attempts to jolt patients into having seizures involved injecting them with chemicals. "The problem was that the chemicals used also had bad side effects, including necrosis [death of living cells or tissues] of the muscle," explains Dr. Scheftner. "Also, you never knew how long after the injection a patient would have a seizure. It could be five minutes or ten hours, which made chemical induction an iffy proposition."

The use of ECT as a more regular treatment for depression didn't catch on until after World War II. "It was at that point that this form of shock treatments for depression for various otherwise untreatable conditions came about, and from there, it became increasingly more popular."[241]

By 1945, American psychiatric hospitals were widely using electroshock procedures. At the time, many psychiatrists recognized the potential benefits of the treatment in some patients, noting that when ECT worked, it had an immediate effect on the patient with few side effects. However, administering ECT had its dangers such as too strong convulsions, which could result in broken bones, broken teeth, or a bitten tongue. "A few patients complained of some memory loss, though this usually appeared to be short-term. Many patients, particularly those who had suffered severe, prolonged, and crippling depression, improved dramatically."[242]

IMPROVEMENTS LEAD TO WIDER ACCEPTANCE

Despite a rocky beginning, ECT came back into favor during the latter part of the twentieth century and the first part of the twenty-first century following a variety of improvements that reduced its risks. However, the fact that ECT was given to some patients in the 1950s and '60s without their informed consent contributed to the treatment's controversial reputation.

In the 1950s and '60s, doctors could order the procedure for their hospitalized patients without their consent, and families could likewise request the treatment when committing relatives to mental institutions. This practice was prohibited by the 1974 National Research Act, which established the medical policy of "informed consent." According to Alex Groberman in his article, "Shock Treatments for Depression," "one of the most well-known standards of modern ECT is 'informed consent.' As per the [U.S.] Surgeon General, the only time involuntary shock treatments for depression is permitted is in the extreme cases when all other options have been exhausted. Or, of course, if it is deemed that the ECT can be potentially life-saving."[243]

The medical community worked to try to decrease the risks associated with shock therapy during the latter years of the twentieth century, when doctors began to perform the procedure with anesthesia and under carefully monitored conditions. This substantially reduced the risks of the most worrisome side effects from earlier years, such as memory loss and physical injuries from the seizures. "ECT is much safer today and is given to people while they're under general anesthesia. ... Although ECT still causes some side effects, it now uses electrical currents given in a controlled setting to achieve the most benefit with the fewest possible risks."[244]

During the 1990s, ECT began to be used with a much lower voltage to avoid memory loss or memory distortion. As author

Jonathan Engel found in researching his book, *American Therapy*, "patients who submitted to a full regimen of ten to fifteen treatments recovered rapidly from severe depression ... One patient described his experience[:] 'It is a nonentity, a nothing. You go to sleep, and when you wake up, it is all over. It is easier to take than going to the dentist.'"[245]

WHEN ECT IS AN EFFECTIVE TREATMENT

What makes patients agree to ECT? The effectiveness of the treatment in giving depressed people immediate relief from their symptoms. "Bilateral ECT [which places the electrodes on both temples] works in roughly 70 to 80 percent of all depressions," points out Dr. Scheftner. "Unilateral ECT [which places one electrode on the crown of the head, the other on either the right or left temple] appears to be somewhat less effective, given the current devices we have."

The Consortium for Research in ECT research study found an 87 percent remission rate among severely depressed patients who received shock therapy. The study also found that ECT decreased the chance of relapse as effectively as the use of antidepressant medications when the patients followed up with additional ECT treatments.[246] The consortium notes that shock therapy "often works when other treatments are unsuccessful. ... ECT can provide rapid, significant improvements in severe symptoms of a number of mental health conditions." [247]

Today, ECT is considered a generally safe procedure with minimal risks of side effects, such as confusion, memory loss, nausea, headaches, jaw and/or muscle pain, heart rate and/or blood pressure changes, and complications from receiving anesthesia. "The mortality from the procedure itself is from general anesthetic," says Dr. Scheftner. "Particularly for elderly patients there appears to be some evidence that those with significant depression—enough to bring them to a hospital—who have ECT enjoy a longer lifespan than those with a similar severe depression."

CHANGING THE BRAIN'S CHEMISTRY

Medical professionals still aren't sure exactly why shock therapy relieves depression, but they do know that ECT changes the brain's chemistry in a way that quickly reverses the symptoms of depression. "No one knows for certain how ECT helps treat severe depression and other mental illnesses. What is known, though, is that many chemical aspects of brain function are changed during and after seizure activity. These chemical changes may build upon one another, somehow reducing symptoms of severe depression or other mental illnesses. That's why ECT is most effective in people who receive a full course of multiple treatments."[248]

Depressed people can undergo shock therapy either in a hospital or on an outpatient basis. During each procedure, an electrical current goes from electrodes placed on patients' skulls to their brains, causing a seizure that lasts under a minute. The anesthetic and muscle relaxant keeps the patient calm and unaware of the seizure.[249] "In the United States, ECT treatments are generally given two to three times weekly for three to four weeks—for a total of six to twelve treatments. The number of treatments you'll need depends on the severity of your symptoms and how rapidly they improve."[250]

"We'd gone through everything with Mark, and he'd get a mediocre response or a modest response," says Dr. Scheftner. "We were in a position with his depression that we had to go to something which continues to be the most certain of all treatments for major depression: electric convulsive therapy."

When Dr. Scheftner first broached the subject of ECT as a treatment option, I was a bit nervous, but I was in a bad state of depression, and the traditional methods of treating it with medication weren't working. This was the worse depression I'd ever had. Treatments that had worked before didn't now, and even the new medications had no effect. That's when shock therapy came up.

Most people when they hear about ECT are nervous because of how it has been portrayed in the movies. For me, I frankly didn't have much of a choice if I wanted to recover from this depression. I agreed to try it, especially because my sisters and my father were very supportive. My sisters took me to the treatments. I received the ECT treatments as an outpatient under a twilight sedative. I had a succession of them about once a week, plus talk therapy to help with my ruminations.

Testimonies abound of patients who experience remission or relief from depression after ECT. However, no one quite knows how this happens. Researchers and doctors have provided a multitude of theories but none can agree which one makes the most sense. "The seizure could be key, or shutting off the process that produces seizures. It could center around the electricity, or the same biochemical reactions that make antidepressants work. Many patients prefer to think of ECT as somehow resetting the brain when it gets out of balance, the same way rebooting a balky computer sometimes fixes it."[251]

Other theories about how it works include the idea that inducing an epileptic seizure "can stop even the most severe depression suddenly and completely, likely because seizures naturally release an immediate flood of serotonin, norepinephrine, and dopamine into the brain. Seizures also release brain-healing BDNF [brain-derived neurotrophic factor], which repairs stress-damaged brain cells and causes new brain cells to be born and proliferate in areas of the brain that have been damaged by unipolar major depression."[252]

Although shock therapy usually leads to some immediate relief of depression symptoms, it doesn't cure depression, so follow-up treatments of some kind are necessary. Most patients who experience ECT notice an improvement after a few treatments. "Full improvement may take longer. Response to antidepressant medications, in comparison, can take several weeks or more. Even after your symptoms improve, you'll still need ongoing treatment to prevent a recurrence. ... Known as maintenance therapy, that ongoing treatment doesn't have to be ECT, but it can be. More often, it includes antidepressants or other medications, or psychological counseling (psychotherapy)."[253]

THE EVOLUTION OF ECT

Because shock therapy is still proving to be an effective treatment for severe depression, and methods for the procedure continue to improve, it will likely remain a solid treatment choice for depressed people in the years to come. "It is counterintuitive to see a treatment as time-consuming and tangled as ECT catch on in this era of Prozac and the quick fix. ... Most surprising of all, ECT is the only remedy in mainstream medicine that is expanding in use, receiving increased attention in research, and offering life-saving hope to tens of thousands of people, even as much as the public believes it is extinct."[254]

Looking toward the future, some unanswered questions about shock therapy still remain. Researchers are still searching for answers as to why ECT relieves the symptoms of depression. "Questions also remain about the price shock patients pay in memories lost, in rare cases permanently, and whether such risks can be minimized or eliminated entirely. The rise, fall, and rise again of ECT remains an epic without an ending, as practitioners and potential patients alike wait to see if hopes for success are sustained."[255]

According to Dr. Scheftner, "while memory problems can occur with ECT, there are very few medical problems that prevent the use of ECT. I think most people would choose a further interesting life after ECT than continue to suffer from depression."

Whatever happened with the ECT worked with me because it cleared the cobwebs from my mind. Within a year of starting ECT treatments, I was operating on a different, better level. Not only was I well, but I was thinking more clearly and interested in many more things. My mind was questioning, I could synthesize information very quickly, and come to deductions about personal and business decisions like never before.

After the treatments, I broadened my learning and interests to encompass new areas in life, including politics, world affairs, travel, culture, and entrepreneurship. I was on the family company's board, and began giving back philanthropically and living by the Golden Rule by being a good person and helping people wherever I could. I realized that many of us are so busy in our lives (self-centered and self-absorbed) that we miss easy opportunities to help people on a daily basis. It's not just about money; it's about helping someone when they need it. So I started looking for ways to help others, such as assisting an older person to put their walker in the trunk of his or her car, opening a door for someone at a restaurant, or helping someone jumpstart a car on a cold winter's day. Simple stuff that's easy for all of us to think about and do.

This lingering stigma about shock treatments may keep some depressed people from talking about the option with their doctors. As more people like me talk about their success with ECT, my hope is that more depressed people will be able to experience the hope of a renewed life after undergoing electroconvulsive therapy.

Chapter 13

Talk Therapy and Depression

"Negative thinking patterns can be immensely deceptive and per-suasive, and change is rarely easy. But with patience and persistence, I believe that nearly all individuals suffering from depression can improve and experience a sense of joy and self-esteem once again."
—David D. Burns, Stanford University professor and author of *Feeling Good: The New Mood Therapy*

OVER THE YEARS, DOCTORS AND OTHERS HAVE FOUND THAT therapy—talk, animal/dog, and exercise—can be extremely beneficial to people with depression, especially when accompanied by medication and other treatments. One of the most popular forms of therapy for depression is talk therapy (also called counseling), in which depressed people talk about their thoughts and feelings with others (such as psychiatrists, clinical social workers, psychologists, and support-group members) with the goal of managing or recovering from the disease. Every form of talk therapy focuses in some way on helping depressed people understand how they can tap into the power of their minds to heal.

What's vital about talk therapy is that it helps a patient to recognize patterns of thinking that might hinder the person's recovery. When a patient becomes aware of those patterns, he or she can choose how to respond to the thoughts or "diminish the power thoughts have over your mood and life. This transformation allows you to evaluate behaviors objectively. We become aware of the mental processes that are driving our behavior. Then we have the opportunity to look objectively at those thoughts or feelings, and decide whether we want to respond in our habitual way or try something new."[256]

"Sometimes through talk therapy alone, people with mild to moderate depression improve," said Bonnie Senner,[257] an integrative psychodynamic therapist in the Chicago area. "Talk therapy works for these people when the depression stems from the current situation or when the past colors how they view the world and relate to others. Patients gain insight into how the past is impacting the present, leaving them in a stronger place when the depression lifts. Depressions that have a biological origin frequently need medication in addition to talk therapy. I recommend early in treatment that people get a psychiatric evaluation to see if medication is indicated, or if the medication their internist prescribed is the best one. I often refer them to a psychopharmacologist, who has an expertise in medication management."

Although there's a plethora of different types of talk therapy available from counselors, the two types that have proven to be the most effective (and are also most commonly used) are cognitive therapy (which also is called cognitive behavioral therapy, or CBT) and interpersonal therapy. "CBT focuses on looking at how negative thought patterns may be affecting your mood. The therapist helps you learn how to make positive changes in your thoughts and behaviors. Interpersonal therapy focuses on how you relate to others and helps you make positive changes in your personal relationships. Both types of therapy can be effective in treating depression."[258]

Choosing which type of therapy to pursue—for example, cognitive, interpersonal, psychodynamic therapy (focuses on the past), or family therapy (focuses on relationships)—involves figuring out what your personal goals are for recovery, then discussing the specifics of your depression experience with a therapist with whom you may potentially develop a counseling relationship. During the first session, the therapist will ask detailed questions about those goals, including why you are seeking help and what you hope to accomplish through therapy. "For example, are you looking for ways to better deal with personal relationships, or are you hoping to set goals for yourself and make changes? It's helpful to be as honest as you can with your therapist about your depression and your goals for therapy. After listening to your situation, the therapist should be able to tell you what type of treatment he [or she] recommends and come up with a treatment plan for you."[259]

Remember that more than one approach might be helpful in your recovery. "Talk therapy along with medication can help with depression," says Senner. "Patients feel heard and understood because you develop a relationship with them. It can pull them out of the depression as they feel heard and understood, especially in a time when the rest of the world isn't understanding them."

COGNITIVE THERAPY

Using cognitive therapy, people who are suffering from depression can learn how to transform negative thoughts into positive thoughts that promote healing. The most common approach is with CBT, which many therapists use when treating depressed patients.[260]

Cognitive therapists act like coaches when working with patients. The behavioral component centers on the exact steps the patient can do, such as utilizing a relaxation technique or adding fun activities to their calendar. The cognitive aspect examines the patient's usual thought patterns and delves into how those patterns could elongate or stifle the episode. Then solutions to overcoming those patterns are discussed. "The therapist is like a coach, helping you master both the cognitive and behavioral skills. Just as if you were learning to play soccer or the violin, great emphasis is placed on *practice*."[261]

The process of changing ingrained thought patterns requires sustained effort from patients. There are many different cognitive therapy techniques to assist in that transformation. "Perhaps the most important is the questioning and testing of thoughts, assumptions, and beliefs to determine whether they are realistic. The aim is to identify inaccurate thoughts that may result in depression and subsequently counter these thinking patterns with objective evidence."[262]

Cognitive therapy has been widely tested in research studies—perhaps more so than any other type of talk therapy—and proven to be effective by those studies. I had actually gone to see a talk therapist for another reason when I became engulfed with depression. My therapist then took on the role of support with talk therapy during my depression. I think she probably took the burden off my siblings and my father because I was talking more to her than to them during the episode. Because she was a professional, she was better able to help me get through the depression because she knew how to deal with it.

"Like many talk therapists, I help patients gain insights into how their past is impacting their present, which leaves them in a stronger place when the depression lifts," adds Senner. "That is why talk therapy can be so beneficial to depressed patients."

COGNITIVE THERAPY AND ANTIDEPRESSANTS

Studies, including several rather large ones, have found cognitive therapy "to be as effective as antidepressant medications for the treatment of mild to moderate depression."[263] One of those studies was conducted by Robert J. DeRubeis, Greg J. Siegle, and Steven D. Hollon, who wrote that "cognitive therapy is as efficacious as antidepressant medications at treating depression, and it seems to reduce the risk of relapse even after its discontinuation. Cognitive therapy and antidepressant medication probably engage some similar neural mechanisms, as well as mechanisms that are distinctive to each."[264]

Medication is often thought of as the first approach to try for depression treatment, but CBT can prove more useful in the long term. "Studies that look at the combination of medication and CBT suggest that people get a faster start, feeling better after twelve weeks or so on medication plus CBT, but that in the long run, many people do well utilizing CBT methods without any medication. There is growing evidence that building positive brain circuitry will balance and offset the brain circuits for ruminative, negative thinking, so techniques that enhance feeling centered, spirituality, and positive emotion will be of great value."[265]

The effectiveness of cognitive therapy for treating depression has been found to prevent relapse when treatment has completed. However, patients utilizing medication-alone treatment often need to continue those medicines to prevent a relapse.[266] Cognitive therapy (CT) may be the best overall talk therapy choice for most people with depression. Overall, "CT is a powerful method that can help us change our thinking patterns and feel better emotionally."[267]

"Cognitive behavioral therapy is popular today because it is amenable to research and can be done in a short time period," notes Senner. "But it does not work for everyone. With a new patient who is depressed, I do a thorough evaluation and recommend a psychiatric evaluation as well. A 2010 study[268] showed that psychodynamic therapy was as effective as other evidence-based therapies, but also that the benefits of psychodynamic therapy appeared to be longer lasting."

INTERPERSONAL THERAPY

Depressed people who would like to figure out how to fight depression by improving the quality of their relationships may prefer interpersonal therapy (IPT) instead of cognitive therapy. "IPT is a well-known treatment that has been shown to be as effective as antidepressants in mild to moderate depression. It focuses on a person's relationships and tries to improve the quality of the most important ones."[269]

Just like cognitive therapy, interpersonal therapy has been shown to be effective by many different research studies. IPT zeroes in on problems with interpersonal relationships that could contribute to depression, and also examines problems that depression may cause or exacerbate in relating to others. "Multiple studies have confirmed the effectiveness of IPT for the acute and maintenance treatment of depression. IPT is a time-limited, here-and-now therapy that focuses on developing an understanding of the interpersonal problems in one's life and then developing concrete solutions."[270]

TALKING WITH LOVED ONES

Another way that people suffering from depression can pursue talk therapy is simply by talking with caring, trustworthy friends or family about what they're going through. By engaging in conversations about their illness with those in their personal support group, depressed people can express their thoughts and feelings freely, and hopefully gain some valuable insights that they can use in the healing process.

In my early depressions, I would call my father and siblings to talk. It was extremely helpful to me, but I think it ended up being sometimes overwhelming for them to listen to my ruminations and repetitions.

"Mark would call us all the time," says my sister, Shawn, noting that being a partner in talk therapy can be a challenge. "Depression is a selfish disease because you can become self-absorbed, and you forget that you are calling a young mother with two babies in the middle of the night. It doesn't cross your mind because you're only focused on the fact that you're frightened of something or you've got to work something out. That selfish side is very hard on the family. But at the same time, you [the family member or friend] feel guilty because you don't have it and you wouldn't wish it on anybody. So you do the right thing. And I know it wasn't just me that he called; he called all of my siblings. He may have had us on a rotation. He could have called me at one a.m., another sibling at two a.m., etc. I do know he talked to all of us during his depression episodes."

Of course, turning to personal friends or family for help tends to be a lot less reliably effective than turning to professional therapists because these people haven't usually been specially trained to treat depression. But talk therapy with loved ones can complement professional talk therapy, and for depressed people who, for whatever reason, don't want to pursue professional therapy, talking with friends and family about their depression is better than not talking about it at all.

The support from close friends, family, and the community helps those with depression become more resilient to the world at large. "Social connection helps push the brain in an antidepressant direction, turning down activity in stress circuitry, and boosting the activity of feel-good brain chemicals like dopamine and serotonin. That's why it makes sense to swim hard against the tide of our 'culture of isolation' and to place our relationships at the very top of the priority list. Truly, nothing in life matters more."[271]

Talking with a personal support group provides a valuable sense of community that can have healing benefits simply by pulling depressed people out of isolation. Depressed people can "find authentic community, and the profound sense of belonging it confers"[272] from places of worship, volunteer organizations, social clubs, self-help groups, interest groups, sports leagues, and their workplaces.

Although loved ones will likely give depressed people lots of encouragement, that isn't the most effective tact to help fight the illness. What is? Simply distracting them away from the struggle with depression and toward fun social activities. Reassuring a depressed person rarely triggers a better outlook in the patient because the positive words clash "so sharply with the depressed individual's negative self-view that [they are] dismissed almost immediately. Ironically, the best way to combat depressive feelings of insecurity is often to ignore them, to divert attention instead to more engaging social activities that have the power to lift mood and shift the brain into a less negative mode of thinking."[273]

For those who might not have a circle of friends or family to assist in talk therapy, some countries are exploring peer-support groups or training elders to aid people suffering from depression. In Zimbabwe, for example, three hundred elders have been trained to sit on a park bench outside a clinic and talk through problems with patients. "On any given afternoon in the capital of Harare and nearby cities, an elder woman can be found on a bench outside a clinic, listening intently to another person's stories."[274] With research supporting the efficacy of "social-support methods of care"[275] in treating mental illnesses, having someone trained and waiting to listen can provide the safety net people need.

ACTIVE PARTICIPATION

Depressed people who participate as actively as possible in talk therapy can maximize its benefits. William Marchand, in his book

Depression and Bipolar Disorder: Your Guide to Recovery, puts it this way: "I like the analogy of working with a coach to develop athletic ability. No matter how good the coach is, no improvement in skills will occur without lots of practice. Sitting in a therapist's office once a week is likely to have limited benefit unless it is accompanied by effort on a daily basis to implement changes."[276]

Patients who listen to encouragement from their therapists to stay motivated can experience good outcomes from talk therapy. "Initially, [the patient's] treatment will focus on finding motivation that you can hang onto, and it will progress no faster than [the patient's] mental energy can allow. The close observation and continuing assessment of the therapist can promote that motivation."[277]

PATIENCE

Talk therapy isn't a "quick fix" for depressed patients. "Depression, especially major depression, can take a very long time to lift," points out Senner.

It can take time to experience the full benefits of talk therapy, as it involves a gradual process of talking about your thoughts and feelings, and figuring out the best ways to change negative patterns to overcome depression. You may need to change therapists a few times until you find one whose approach is a good match for you.

So it's important to be patient while you work on healing through talk therapy and discover what works best for you. For example, what really benefited me was just sitting down with my therapist and talking about how things were going, especially if I had a bad day. It helped that we were able to talk about more than just my depression.

Over time, those with depression will start to notice improvement in moods or relationships with others. "If you aren't feeling any better, talk with your therapist. [He or] she may be able to try another approach to therapy or refer you for other kinds of treatment. Or you might benefit from seeing someone else. You may need to see more than one therapist to find the type of therapy that's right for you. Therapy is not always easy and can sometimes even be painful as you work through difficult problems. But if you stick with it, talk therapy can also be gratifying and rewarding—and can give you the tools you need to help ease your depression."[278]

Chapter 14

Animal Therapy and Depression

"In a way, we could all use a psychiatric service or therapy dog because of the incredible amount of stress that we're all under."
    –Dr. Carole Lieberman, American psychiatrist

HEALING FROM DEPRESSION MAY COME IN THE FORM OF A DOG'S wagging tail and sloppy kiss, a cat's soft snuggle and loud purr, or a bird's playful antics and cheerful song. Animals, whose companionship has comforted humans throughout history, can sometimes play important roles in the healing process for depressed people.

"The earliest reported use of pets as therapy[279] occurred in eighteenth-century England," says Callandre Cozzolino,[280] executive director of Canine Therapy Corps in Chicago. "The first documented usage in the United States was in New York during World War II."

Dogs and other pets might not have been formally used as therapy until recently in this country, but domesticated animals have long been living with humans, bringing them solace and companionship.

A DOG'S LIFE

Dogs have been domesticated animals and living as part of the community with humans for thousands of years.[281] The bond between humans and dogs can be unbreakable. "The ability and intuition of dogs coupled with their enthusiasm and lust for life really make them suitable for making us feel better, which is the purpose of animal therapy," notes Cozzolino.

Canines provide comfort and friendship to all who own them, but it's only been rather recently that dogs have been trained to assist in a depressed person's therapy and rehabilitation. "Service and assistance dogs have been helping owners have more freedom to accomplish more on their own for years," says Cozzolino. "But only lately have we realized how the amazing companionship dogs offer can be translated into helping people with depression and other mental illnesses get better."

The rise of canines as service animals became formalized after World War I.[282] However, in the early days of dogs being used for therapy, there was a reluctance to have the animals in public-health settings, like a hospital. "It was quite the paradigm shift of risk versus reward to get doctors and others in the medical field to accept the small risk of having animals in a hospital setting," says Cozzolino. "The positive, therapeutic value of having animals there to help the patients in their recovery outweighs any of the risks, which are low."

Canine Therapy Corps works with institutions like hospitals to establish dog-therapy programs. "We help those places establish protocols for the dogs, such as using only one entrance/exit, putting a sheet down if the dog will be on a chair or bed, having plenty of hand sanitizer available, etc. These make the visits less risky and improve the time spent with the patients," explains Cozzolino.

The very act of caring for animals can be therapeutic in and of itself. "Pets have an almost magical ability to increase our sense of wellbeing through their affectionate physical contact, which lowers stress hormones and boosts the activity of feel-good brain chemicals like dopamine and serotonin. Pets also provide us with a faithful source of social companionship, and a deep feeling that we truly *matter*: They literally depend on us for their very lives."[283]

Research into the benefits of animal therapy continues, but studies so far suggest that depressed people can gain myriad healing benefits from spending time with animals. "Benefits may include enhanced socialization; reduced levels of stress, anxiety, and loneliness; improved mood; and development of recreation skills. … There is some preliminary evidence that having an animal friend may support your recovery."[284]

Studies have found that animals lower tension and improve a person's overall mood, but the primary benefit may be unconditional love. That unconditional love can give those with depression hope and comfort.

Cozzolino has found that a patient's mood can improve from just one visit from a dog. "Petting a dog can lower a person's resting heart rate and for those in a recovery room after an operation, a therapy dog reduces the need for pain medication," she says. "That simple touch has many benefits."

In addition, the available evidence suggests that depressed people who have dogs involved in their therapy work longer and harder at their own recovery. "It gives them a distraction from their own thoughts," says Cozzolino. "A dog makes repetitive tasks seem less repetitive and more fun, such as tossing a ball by yourself versus tossing a ball to a dog."

Benefits of animal therapy include:

- **Simple love.** If your relationships with family and friends are difficult and unraveled, a pet can provide the antidote to feelings of frustration and of being unloved. Pets don't get hurt feelings or give unwanted advice. Pets allow people to just be as they are.

- **Responsibility.** The idea of taking care of another living thing may seem too hard for a person with depression, especially when taking care of oneself is challenging. But experts point out that increasing a person's responsibility, such as with a pet, provides new focus to the life of a depressed person.
- **Activity.** Depression can make it hard for someone to get the physical activity we all need. Pets can provide the impetus to get moving. Dogs need to be walked, and even cats, fish, and birds have needs that can give a person a reason to get up and about.
- **Routine.** Pets offer a person with depression a built-in daily schedule—which can be lifesaving. Most domestic animals have natural habits—such as waking the owner up in the morning and being persistent in demanding walks and food—that provides a person with daily structure.
- **Companionship.** By its very nature, depression tends to isolate those who suffer from it. Depressed people often pull back from family and friends, but a pet means the person is never alone.
- **Social interaction.** Pets can gently nudge their owners into more social contact, such as chatting with fellow dog walkers while at the park or visiting with other pet owners while waiting at the vet. Pets offer a natural icebreaker with other human beings.
- **Touch.** Studies have found that we feel better when we have physical contact with others, and pets offer the opportunity to touch that is good for us. Petting cats or dogs can sooth frazzled emotions and lower heart rates.

- **Better health.** Research has shown that dog owner-
  ship lowers stress hormones, reduces blood pressure,
  and lifts feel-good chemicals in the brain.

Which pet should you choose to help in the fight against depression? Dogs are by nature social animals and may be an especially good choice for depressed people interested in pursuing animal therapy. Dogs deliver unconditional love in an enthusiastic manner. "They don't care if we have a bad hair day or aren't in the best mood; our canine companions will always be there for us. Of course, other animals can also be great companions, but I think the love that dogs have for humans is a great example of what we can get from our furry friends."[285]

Cats are popular animal-therapy choices, too, because they also like to snuggle and play with their human companions. But if adopting a dog or cat isn't practical—for example, if you're allergic or concerned about the cost and time needed for their care—other animals also can be helpful companions to people with depression. "Birds can be surprisingly affectionate. ... While you may not want to snuggle with a fish or a turtle, caring for them could also improve your mood. It creates responsibility and a new focus. Studies have shown that watching fish can lower your pulse and ease muscle tension too."[286]

By all accounts, we will uncover more uses for pet therapy in the years to come as a greater number of doctors and health-care professionals see the benefits of dogs and other animals in healing humans. "Some therapists incorporate pet therapy into their counseling sessions, allowing patients to stroke or cuddle a dog while working through issues with the counselor," says Cozzolino. "That can help patients relax in therapy and open up, resulting in an increased willingness to share important information with their therapists."

Dogs for certified therapy don't require the task-based training of a service animal. "There is also another category of dogs separate and distinct [from] service animals and therapy animals called emotional support animals. Emotional support animals can simply be well-behaved pets, and they are allowed to live with their owners," explains Cozzolino.

She sees a bright future for pet therapy as more hospitals are beginning to allow dogs on the floor to help patients in their recovery and more psychologists are using dogs or recommending patients get dogs to assist in the healing process. "There is a lot more to be done in this area, but as more studies are done, I'm sure pet therapy will grow to become an accepted form of depression treatment," says Cozzolino.

Dog Therapy in Action

Canine Therapy Corps works with groups of people with mental illness and substance abuse, as well as with military veterans. One effective program is a dog-handling class that lasts between six and ten weeks. "They're expected to be here every week, which can be challenging," says Callandre Cozzolino, executive director of the Chicago-based organization.

The program teaches participants perseverance, patience, how to maintain a positive attitude, and how to break down a task into manageable pieces. One of the exercises that helps accomplish this goal is dog agility. Participants navigate a small agility course with their therapy dog. Participants prepare mentally by memorizing the course, but they also have to be able to stay positive and connected to their dog even if they make a mistake. Of course, they also are encouraged to have lots of fun while working with the dogs.

"Many after a session will tell us how much better they feel," says Cozzolino. "It's given them a reprieve from their life and they leave feeling a little bit more rejuvenated."

Chapter 15

Exercise and Depression

"Exercise is probably the single most-effective depression-defeater you can do."

—Margaret Wehrenberg, American author of
The 10 Best-Ever Depression Management Techniques

EXERCISING BENEFITS THE BRAIN IN SO MANY WAYS THAT exercise therapy for depression may be one of the best treatments. The two types of exercise that studies have shown are most effective in fighting depression—aerobic exercise and yoga—are fairly easy to incorporate into people's daily lives. But while many depression patients know that exercising is good for them, they often have trouble actually doing the exercise, because depression saps people's energy and motivation.

Studies have shown that physical activity at a higher level can correspond with lower depression levels. "Further, a fairly large body of literature suggests that aerobic exercise may be associated with reduced depressive symptoms. There is also some evidence for the benefits of nonaerobic exercise. Reviews of the evidence published in scientific journals generally conclude that exercise is beneficial for depression."[287]

"Exercise is important for overall mental stability," says Zak Rivera,[288] a personal trainer with Focused Results in Lake Bluff,

Illinois. "Exercise gives people a sense of purpose and direction. I've noticed that when someone comes in for a training session dragging a little bit that after the workout, the majority of the time, they are smiling—even though they are dripping with sweat and tired."

People can quickly reap the benefits of exercise as a treatment for depression. "Exercise is extraordinarily important for maintaining both physical and mental health. Aerobic exercise is the most potent antidepressant activity ever discovered, with the ability to reverse the toxic effects of depression on the brain. Physical activity even has mood-elevating effects that can usually be felt in a matter of minutes."[289]

A BRAIN CHANGER

Because exercise changes the activity of brain chemicals just like medication does, it can be as powerful in treating the disease as antidepressants, although medications should be used along with an exercise routine in most depression cases. "Medication isn't the only way to correct brain abnormalities in depression. Physical exercise also brings about profound changes in the brain—changes that rival those seen with the most potent antidepressant medications."[290]

Exercise literally changes the brain, similar to what happens when taking antidepressant medicines. Exercise bumps up the activity of dopamine and serotonin, important chemicals in our brain that can get off track by depression. "It also stimulates the brain's release of a key growth hormone (BDNF), which in turn helps reverse the toxic, brain-damaging effects of depression. It even sharpens memory and concentration, and helps us think more clearly. Simply put, *exercise is medicine*—one that affects the brain more powerfully than any drug."[291]

"Exercise gets the endorphins going—those feel-good hormones moving inside your body," notes Rivera. "It also gives people a goal. When they make an appointment with me, it keeps them accountable. As the workouts progress, they see their body and stamina changing too."

Like SSRI medications (see Chapter 9 for more on these medicines), exercise increases the serotonin levels in the brain, albeit in different ways. "Exercise … may affect serotonin levels more positively in people who have problems with serotonin, as seen in research with depressed persons. … Exercise also enhances BDNF to encourage the production of new brain cells that can produce serotonin. Additionally, it increases blood flow to the brain, which is associated with many aspects of brain health, and it can affect your neurotransmitter levels as well as the overall functioning of parts of the brain."[292]

AEROBIC EXERCISE

The best type of exercise to fight depression is aerobic exercise, which a variety of research studies have shown to be more effective at reducing depression symptoms than any other form of exercise. Researchers think that aerobic exercise works against depression by releasing endorphin hormones in the body that help grow back parts of the brain that have shrunk due to depression. "Researchers have … consistently observed a powerful therapeutic benefit from *aerobic* exercise—the kind of workout that causes your heart rate to stay elevated for several minutes at a time."[293] Common aerobic exercises are running or jogging, fast walking, swimming, biking, hiking, dancing, stair climbing, racquetball or tennis, and team sports.

Rivera utilizes boxing and kickboxing along with SlamBall (a form of basketball played with four trampolines in front of each net and boards around the court edge). "There's something about boxing or SlamBall that's empowering and that can help a person get out any negative energy," he says. "However, any exercise will get those positive feelings going."

The effects of aerobic exercise on depression are still being studied. However, it appears that the power of aerobic exercise to release endorphins is most likely what makes it such a successful treatment. "The endorphin hypothesis suggests that exercise releases endorphin neurotransmitters, which results in the decrease of depressive symptoms."[294]

Aerobic exercise also treats depression by reducing stress. "Exercise is a prime stress reliever. ... For the depressed person with a lot of agitation, physical activities are better sources of stress relief than sitting still. Aerobic exercise is best, because it is a great long-term relaxer."[295]

When depressed people are doing aerobic exercise they enjoy, their minds can move away from the negative thoughts and toward positive thoughts that promote healing. "Time really does fly when we're caught up in something enjoyable, even when there's physical exercise involved."[296]

The simplest way to get aerobic exercise—walking—is easy to start doing and a good choice for depressed people who are struggling with low energy and motivation. "Walking has the absolute best record for easy access. ... The director of the Bipolar Clinic associated with Harvard, Dr. Gary Sachs, says, 'Here's your exercise program: go to the door, look at your watch. Walk 7.5 minutes in any direction, then turn around and walk home. Do that five days a week at least.'"[297] Walking is the best antidepressant form of exercise because "our bodies are designed for it—and because it's something just about everyone can do."[298]

So how much aerobic exercise should depressed people try to do? No official standards have been set yet, but health experts recommend between 90 and a 105 minutes of aerobic exercise a week to produce an antidepressant effect on depression patients.[299]

"I like to see my clients at least two or three times a week because that ensures if they happen to miss one workout, they have another scheduled fairly soon," says Rivera, who recommends at least six hours of aerobic activity weekly.

What's most important is simply getting started with any amount of aerobic exercise. Then, depressed people can gradually work up to meeting greater exercise goals. "Educate yourself on the importance of exercise. Find a type of exercise you enjoy. What opportunities do you have to do it? Decide the largest possible step you can reasonably take in the direction of exercise. Get a partner if possible. Commit to an action plan. Be accountable. Keep track of what you do. Evaluate your progress and increase your goal regularly until you hit your target for the prescription for exercise."[300]

YOGA

Yoga is a lower-impact form of exercise that researchers have found effective in depression treatment. Yoga fights depression through the endorphin-releasing benefits of physical exercise as well as the positive-thinking benefits of mindfulness. "Although aerobic exercise is good ... yoga is another means of promoting mental health."[301]

Daily yoga practice has been said to bring a person's physical body and emotions back into balance. "You will feel more energy, love yourself more, and have a happier life."[302]

Yoga's distinctive message to people who feel broken by their depression is that they are still whole as human beings—and when they choose to focus on their wholeness, their depression will be reduced. "Even beneath ... the agony of depression, yoga says, you are whole. ... When you step onto your yoga mat, you are reminded of that wholeness, and the practice clears a pathway through your symptoms to the ground of your being, that which is your natural state."[303] In addition, depression often produces a feeling that the person is separated from himself, wondering, "What is wrong with me?" Yoga approaches from the opposite perspective of "What is right with me?"[304]

People can't do yoga without concentrating on the poses, thus shifting their focus away from depression and toward something positive. "The highs, lows, the extremes of all the emotions are brought into balance by the physical practice, and the mind is soothed by the philosophy."[305] Each yoga stage relieves the practitioner from obsessed and negative thoughts. "To learn the pose your mind must focus on the details of alignment. Later, when you're in the pose and you allow your mind to become absorbed in the sensations in your body, you are very far from your everyday troubles."[306]

To use yoga to treat depression, patients should practice regularly with a qualified teacher as well as self-practice daily as well. "Simple spinal flexes on your hands and knees, a twist, a mountain pose, remembering to breathe long and deep through your nostrils, may be a good beginning."[307]

Overall, any exercise can have a positive impact on depressed patients. Remember to consult with your regular doctor before starting any exercise.

Putting Personal Trainers into Play

Personal training came into vogue during the first half of the twentieth century in America, although various cultures—including Greek and Roman—did have fitness training for athletic events and warfare in ancient times. Jack LaLanne, a fitness and nutritional expert who opened what many deem the first health club in the United States in 1936,[308] is often credited with popularizing personal training.

In 1954, the American College of Sports Medicine in Indianapolis was founded with the goal of promoting health and fitness, and providing certification for fitness professionals, including personal trainers. But it took until the 1980s for personal trainers as a career to take off.

Here are some things to consider when thinking about working with a personal trainer to help alleviate depression symptoms. Remember to consult your physician before beginning any exercise program.

- **Health history.** A personal trainer takes a full health history questionnaire of all clients to discuss anything that might limit the person's ability to exercise. This includes talking about what medications the client is taking, as some medicines can cause dehydration or increase blood pressure.
- **Customization.** A personal trainer assesses the client's fitness level at the beginning, and helps the client set reasonable and attainable goals with a personalized workout routine.
- **Accountability.** Meeting with a personal trainer versus going to the gym or working out alone provides a layer of responsibility that can be particularly helpful for a depressed person who might have trouble getting out of bed some days. Sometimes knowing that someone is waiting for you can be motivating.

Here are some things to keep in mind when choosing a personal trainer:

- **Certification.** Today personal trainers can be certified through the American College of Sports Medicine, the Aerobic and Fitness Association of America, or the National Academy of Sports Medicine. "Looking for the gold standard of certification from a reputable organization like these three will ensure that your trainer has been properly trained," says Zak Rivera, a personal trainer with Focused Results in Lake Bluff, Illinois. "There are a lot of trainers who treat everyone the same, but especially for someone with a mental illness like depression, you want a trainer who will pay close attention to your feelings and your goals in order to empower you to be the best person you can be."

- **Trial run.** Be sure to ask for a free trial session before signing up with a personal trainer to ensure a good fit. "You want a good connection with your trainer because they will get you to a better place physically and mentally," notes Rivera.

- **Honesty.** You want someone with whom you can be honest about the workout and anything that could impact your exercise. "If you can't be honest with your personal trainer, we can't help you," says Rivera. "We want to have a dialogue with our clients in order to be in the best position to assist them in reaching their goals."

- **Environment.** Make sure the location and atmosphere of the gym is one that is inviting to you. "When people come to our gym, we want them to feel like they're walking into their home," says Rivera. "We also don't have mirrors because we found them to be distracting to our clients in a negative way. Instead, we put up on our walls positive, inspiring, and thoughtful words to give our clients encouragement."

Overall, a personal trainer can be a great partner for depressed people in working toward their full recovery. "The key to fitness is to always keep your eyes on the end result because that will keep you moving," says Rivera.

Chapter 16

Nutrition and Depression

"Maybe you have to know the darkness before you can appreciate the light."

—Madeleine L'Engle, American author

In recent years, the role of nutrition in relation to disease and health has become more prominent, with research and studies finding that eating right can have a positive impact on overall health.

Just as nutrition is important in fighting many other types of disease, it also appears to be a key factor in trying to prevent and heal depression. But as with medications, "the story behind diet and depression is complex."[309] Poor nutrition doesn't by itself cause the disease, but it may be a contributing factor in developing depression, and it may make existing depression worse. "A poor diet doesn't cause unipolar major depression, but inadequate nutrition can result in deficiencies of amino acids, fatty acids, vitamins, and minerals that impair your health, upset bodily processes, disturb the function and growth of brain cells, and worsen your depressive symptoms."[310]

Some medical professionals also point out that "nutrition can play a key role in the onset as well as the severity and duration of depression. Many of the easily noticeable food patterns [poor appetite, skipping meals, and a marked preference for sweets] that precede depression are the same as those that occur during depression."[311] Research has discovered several foods have a depression-fighting ability, including omega-3 fatty acids, vitamins, folate, antioxidants, amino acids, and certain minerals.

OMEGA-3 FATTY ACIDS

Omega-3 fatty acids are essential acids found most commonly in fish oils; they play an important role in the brain's functioning processes. As a result, consuming an insufficient amount of omega-3 fatty acids may make people more prone to depression. "When our dietary fats fall out of balance, we become vulnerable to many forms of illness. Depression is one of the most common."[312] A growing body of research supports the fact that omega-3 fats *"have a potent antidepressant effect"* [emphasis in original text].[313]

Research has shown that regularly eating enough omega-3 fatty acids may help prevent and treat depression.[314] Why are omega-3 fatty acids so beneficial in the fight against depression? They reduce inflammation in the body that contributes to depression and help neurotransmitters work properly in the brain, which is crucial for maintaining mental health. Major depression elevates cytokines and eicosanoids, compounds that produce low-level inflammation in brain tissue and other areas in the body. "Antidepressants suppress this harmful activity, but so can increased levels of omega-3s, and probably more efficiently. Finally, in addition to their role in inflammatory processes, the omega-3 fatty acids are also important for proper nerve cell function. ... These fats become part of the nerve cell membrane and are important for keeping the cell and their receptors working efficiently."[315]

Depressed people can take fish-oil capsules to replace essential fatty acids (EFAs), which have been found to help in recovery from the disease.[316] "The two omega-3 fatty acids, eicosapentaenoic acid (EPA), which the body converts into docosahexanoic acid (DHA), found in fish oil, have been found to elicit antidepressant effects in humans. Many of the proposed mechanisms of this conversion involve neurotransmitters."[317]

Omega-3 fatty acids are so effective at fighting depression, in fact, that they "may be your best bet among supplements to help your fight against depression."[318] Because our bodies can't manufacture omega-3s, we must look to our diets to supply these essential fatty acids. Research has shown that omega-3 fatty acids even increase the effectiveness of antidepressants. "Omega-3s appear to reduce inflammation and stabilize cell membranes, similar to some of the new antidepressants that are currently being tested."[319]

Depressed people may want to consider adopting the Mediterranean diet, which research studies has found to be effective at fighting depression because of its emphasis on omega-3 fatty acids. The diet of residents in the Mediterranean area uses an abundance of olive oil, which is "a rich source of monounsaturated fatty acids."[320] A study by the University of Navarra in Pamplona, Spain, linked following the Mediterranean diet with a reduced risk of depression. "The risk for becoming depressed was about twice as high in people who had the lowest adherence to the Mediterranean diet compared with those who had good or strong adherence to this dietary pattern. Other studies have found that people who eat 'Western diets' that are high in processed or 'fast foods,' meats, and other sources of saturated fats have higher rates of depression than those who eat healthier diets."[321]

Eating fish and other foods that contain omega-3 fats can help people in their fight against depression, especially when used in conjunction with other treatments. Fish containing high levels of omega-3s include herring, kippers, salmon, and trout; seafood with lower levels of omega-3s include scallops and shrimp. Other foods containing fatty acids helpful for the diets of depressed patients are currant seed, grape seed, and walnuts.[322]

VITAMINS

Deficiencies in certain types of vitamins have been linked to depression in patients participating in research studies. Although it's not possible to cure depression just by taking vitamins—despite the claims of some advertisers shilling supplements—anyone struggling with depression should ensure that he or she consumes enough of the vitamins necessary for proper brain functioning on a daily basis.

It's best to think of taking vitamins in terms of correcting deficiencies, not as curing the disease. "Although there can be many good reasons for taking vitamins and minerals, research hasn't backed up theories that supplemental vitamins help reduce depression in people who do not have a specific vitamin deficiency. ... Deficiencies of three vitamins—folate, vitamin D, and vitamin B12—have been associated with depression in some, but not all, studies."[323] Depressed people should especially make sure to get enough of vitamins A, B1, B2, B3, B6, B12, C, D, and E, as well as folate.[324]

FOLATE

Out of all vitamins, the one that has been shown in research studies to have the most promise in treating depression is folate (also called folic acid), which is in the B complex vitamin family. Researchers have studied folate extensively to determine how this vitamin can benefit those with depression. "A review of research on folate supplements conducted by Drs. [Maurizio] Fava and [David] Mischoulon at Harvard University ... found evidence for the usefulness of folate augmentation of antidepressants for residual symptoms for depression."[325]

On average, those suffering from depression have folate levels in their bloodstream 25 percent lower than normal, healthy levels. Having such low folate levels has been found to be "a strong predisposing factor of poor outcome with antidepressant therapy. A controlled study has been reported to have shown that 500 mcg of folic acid enhanced the effectiveness of antidepressant medication. Folate's critical role in brain metabolic pathways has been well recognized by various researchers who have noted that depressive symptoms are the most common neuropsychiatric manifestation of folate deficiency."[326]

OTHER B VITAMINS

Besides folate, a variety of other B complex vitamins may help people fight depression. These B vitamins help with stress and depression, while also transforming the brain's amino acids into neurotransmitters like dopamine, norepinephrine, and serotonin. The Bs also keep one's body from developing too much homocysteine (an amino acid), which can cause inflammation.[327]

A key study on the effect of B vitamins on depression found that an increased amount of vitamin B2 and B6 improved the mood of both men and women.[328] Some medical professionals recommend depressed people "either [take] … a B-complex that contains all of the B vitamins or else [look] … for a very good multivitamin with adequate doses of B6, B12, and folic acid."[329]

ANTIOXIDANTS

Antioxidants (molecules that help prevent damage to the body's cells) also help fight depression. The most important antioxidant to consider for promoting good mental health is vitamin C. Some research seems to imply that depression could be tied "to an overly sensitive immune-system response and the excessive inflammation that results. ... Antidepressants seem to work as potent anti-inflammatory drugs—but antioxidants, while less intense, have something of the same effect. They, too, help to dampen the inflammatory response, as well as protecting brain tissue."[330]

Antioxidants help the body best use the other nutrients that also help fight depression. Omega-3 fatty acids need the protection antioxidants provide; taking a 500 milligram vitamin C supplement daily can give the needed protection.[331] A healthful diet also can ensure you get enough of this antioxidant: "Vitamin C is readily available from raw citrus fruits, strawberries, tomatoes, broccoli, and other foods. ...Vitamin C is necessary for the body to produce the serotonin and norepinephrine that help prevent depression."[332]

VITAMIN D

Vitamin D, which is often added to milk, may help people with depression. A study done in Norway linked low vitamin D levels with depression, while those taking a vitamin D supplement found improvement with depression symptoms. "Although routine use of vitamin D for depression is not recommended, it may be a good idea to check for a deficiency in this vitamin if other therapies don't seem to be working or if you are stuck in depression."[333]

AMINO ACIDS

Amino acids, which the body uses to build proteins, help the brain's neurotransmitters (chemicals that transmit messages between the brain's neurons) work properly. Because a major contributing factor to depression is neurotransmitters that don't work well, it's important to consume enough amino acids regularly to fight the disease of depression.

Eating a diet rich in proteins provides amino acids that can help people fight depression. Foods such as dairy products, eggs, meats, and milk should be part of a high-quality protein diet. "Many of the neurotransmitters in the brain are made from amino acids. The neurotransmitter dopamine is made from the amino acid tyrosine and the neurotransmitter serotonin is made from tryptophan. If there is a lack of any of these two amino acids, there will not be enough synthesis of the respective neurotransmitters, which is associated with low mood and aggression in the patients."[334]

Research into the benefits of amino acids has found that methionine, phenylalanine, tyrosine, and tryptophan provide the most benefit in treating depression, among other mood disorders.[335]

MINERALS

Consuming the proper amount of minerals is optimal for brain function. "Some minerals, including calcium and magnesium, are directly involved in processes whereby neurotransmitters affect our cells."[336] Some doctors recommend that depressed people make sure they have enough of the minerals calcium, magnesium, chromium, copper, zinc, and manganese. Other minerals that can promote good mental health include iodine, iron, lithium, and selenium.

Zinc is especially effective at fighting depression, say researchers. "At least five studies have shown that zinc levels are lower in those with clinical depression. Furthermore, intervention research shows that oral zinc can influence the effectiveness of antidepressant therapy."[337]

DIET VERSUS SUPPLEMENTS

Although beneficial nutrients can be found naturally in foods, it's sometimes not practical for people who already suffer from depression to eat well. One of the symptoms of depression is low energy, and it takes energy to make the effort to eat a richly varied and healthful diet. However, taking routine vitamin supplements for depression isn't always the right course of treatment.[338]

Getting all the body's essential nutrients from food is ideal, but that doesn't usually happen, given the realities of how many people eat. "Your brain needs minerals and vitamins to process serotonin, norepinephrine, dopamine, and beta-endorphins, and to stabilize your mood and energy. Ideally, we'd get all the vitamins and minerals we need from the food we eat, but often we simply don't."[339]

Sometimes taking a multivitamin daily can close any nutrition gaps. While food can deliver most of the necessary vitamins, major depression can make eating nutritious food difficult.[340]

The B complex vitamins that help fight depression are included in most multivitamin supplements, so an easy way for people to ensure that they're consuming enough B vitamins every day is simply to take a daily multivitamin. Because antioxidants aren't as potent when consumed outside of their natural form, it's best to eat as many fruits and vegetables as possible to ensure adequate intake of antioxidants. However, getting antioxidants through supplements is better than nothing. "Clearly it is best to get antioxidants from your diet by eating a wide range of fresh fruits and vegetables, particularly those that are bright red, purple, or dark green."[341]

For depressed people with excessive stress or the inability to consume a diet rich in fruits and vegetables, supplementing with vitamin C, vitamin E, beta-carotene, and selenium capsules can be helpful.

Nutrition plays an important role in preventing depression and assisting in recovery from depression. Those with a family history of depression or who have suffered depressive episodes should consider paying close attention to their diets to ensure they are getting the vitamins, minerals, antioxidants, folate, amino acids, and omega-3s necessary for a healthy body and mind. Family members can assist with this by bringing healthy meals to the depressed loved one, or by stocking a freezer with easy-to-prepare foods rich in those nutrients.

Chapter 17

Patients and Depression Treatment

"Getting better from depression demands a lifelong commitment. I've made that commitment for my life's sake and for the sake of those who love me."

—Susan Polis Schutz, American poet and co-founder of Blue Mountain Arts

SOMETIMES A PERSON WILL PUT OFF GETTING TREATMENT FOR depression until the disease incapacitates him or her, having managed until that point to function well enough at work or hide their depression from family members. Or it could be that treatment isn't working as well as it had in the past and the person is reluctant to say so, or doesn't notice.

When I first encountered depression, I just wanted to know what I had and how to get better. After a full diagnostic workup and a psych evaluation, my depression diagnosis was confirmed. Back then (nearly four decades ago), the prescribed medications (lithium and other MAOIs) required twice-weekly blood tests to manage the medicines and track dosage. The side effects were very unpleasant, including constipation, dry mouth, and cravings for sweets.

The biggest thing I appreciated from that initial depression experience was that my doctors educated me about what was happening in my head. That helped me to persevere through the treatment and to trust that the doctors would help me find a way to overcome the depression.

Then I experienced my worst depression at 47 years old. I had been chairman of the Follett company for two years, and prior to that position, I was vice chairman of the family business for two years. This depression lasted two years and the "go-to" medications that had worked before weren't working as effectively. I was working far below my potential; my brother and father were concerned for my health and my job. Because none of the medications were working, I slipped deeper and deeper into my depression.

That's when my brother and father talked with my doctors about trying electroconvulsive therapy. All told, I had five outpatient electroconvulsive therapy sessions. The treatments weren't scary or anything like what movies like *One Flew Over the Cuckoo's Nest* had portrayed in such a negative fashion. Before each session, I was given a twilight sedative and muscle relaxant. When I woke up from each ECT treatment, I hadn't felt a thing. (See Chapter 12 for more information on ECT treatments.)

Shortly after the final ECT treatment, something amazing happened! All the things I had learned in my personal life and all the things I learned in my business life came together. My brain was fully integrated or rewired, and I was smarter than I had ever been. My interests were already varied, but I became a seeker of knowledge in areas I never knew about before. I was interested in world events, politics, and problem solving. My mind was working at warp speed—and it was wonderful!

After experiencing my new self, I realized how lucky I was. I had lost years of my adult life to depression. I made a decision there and then that I wanted to help people who had mental illness by sharing my story and giving them hope. I wanted to encourage them that there is light at the end of the tunnel if you persevere through the illness with the help of your doctors, treatments, and support group of family and friends.

During my last five or six years of being chairman, I was on fire. It was like I was a different person because all my interests were different and more expanded not only in the business but in my personal life as well. The most amazing thing had happened to me and it changed my life. In the whole period of my growing up, my family had to learn with me how to support me and make sure I was supported because of the depression that came and went. My family became proficient in knowing—even when I was ranting and raving because of my obsessive-compulsion or rumination—that it was part of the illness. To calm me down, they knew that they needed to let me rant and rave, and make me realize that some of the things I was so concerned about weren't really major issues.

My family was very supportive and encouraged me to keep with my treatment regimen. Sometimes their efforts worked and sometimes they didn't. It wasn't an easy path back then. With today's medication, you don't have to go in for blood tests and a lot of the side effects have been reduced or eliminated completely.

For others battling depression, it's important to not give up and to do what the doctors order—whether that's medications, animal therapy, talk therapy, exercise, or other treatment. You have a bit of the responsibility even though you're ill. Even though you are feeling sick, you have to go down the pathway in a somewhat logical manner. I think for some people it is difficult to stay on the path, especially when they start feeling better. Sometimes people will stop taking their medications without a doctor's approval, precipitating a slide back into depression that can be even worse than the original episode.

Let me reemphasize that I believe the key to getting well is getting properly diagnosed by a psychopharmacologist at a major teaching hospital if your depression is severe. Stick to your treatment protocol with the doctor. When you are feeling better, don't stop taking the meds. Your doctor will determine in consultation with you when to take you off the medications; you could trigger a relapse if you stop taking your medicines before your doctor gives the okay.

Finally, never give up and persevere! You need to be focused and determined to beat this illness. Be open to new drug protocols and treatments if others don't solve your depression. Your doctors, therapists, and support groups will be there to help you. And remember: You are not alone!

Chapter 18

Families and Depression Treatment

"A lot of people don't realize that depression is an illness. I don't wish it on anyone, but if they would know how it feels, I swear they would think twice before they just shrug it off."
—Jonathan Davis, American musician

OFTEN FAMILY MEMBERS CAN BE OF ENORMOUS HELP TO THOSE suffering from depression—or they can be a hindrance to treatment. Sometimes family members and friends aren't helpful, not because they don't want to assist their loved one in depression treatment, but because they don't know how. Other times family members can get worn down by the cyclical nature of depression, especially if the loved one has experienced more than one round of depression. Groups like the Depression and Bipolar Support Alliance, Mental Health America, and the National Alliance on Mental Illness provide both in-person and online support for families with members suffering from depression. (See the resources section on page 176 for more information.)

The best thing for family members of a depressed loved one is to be as understanding as possible of the disease and the way the person acts while in the midst of an episode or depressive cycle. Some things to keep in mind include:

- **Realize depression is serious.** It's not something a person can overcome on his own. "Family members need to simply acknowledge there is a depression, that this is greater than the unpleasant mood everyone gets when there is a breakup with an important person or your dog dies," says Dr. Scheftner.
- **Know it's not personal.** Someone with depression will likely seem angry and find it hard to show love to others. "Mark wasn't really Mark when he went through the depression episodes," says my sister Robin.
- **Understand the disease.** Mental-health illnesses are among the most misunderstood diseases today, in large part because of the stigma still attached to depression and other mental-health illnesses. "It's hard for someone who hasn't experienced depression to 'get' what the disease does to a person," explains Senner, an integrated psychodynamic therapist. "Initially, I often include the spouse and other close family members of the patient to help them gain a better understanding of depression so they can be supportive in the most beneficial way."
- **Recognize the symptoms.** Just like cancer can zap a person of his or her strength, depression can make a person lethargic and unresponsive to normal things. "If you have a family member who is sad, blue, and down in the dumps, look for changes in appetite and sleep, capacity for concentration and changes in their future outlook," says Dr. Scheftner. "When you start seeing multiple symptoms on that list, including even

comments like 'I wish I were dead,' you need to make your own initial diagnosis that this is a depression that requires evaluation by a medical professional."

- **Encourage treatment.** Hiding the problem won't make it go away, but delaying treatment can be deadly for your loved one, especially if they exhibit any of the signs of suicidal thoughts (see Chapter 1 for details). Also check to make sure a loved one is doing the treatment or taking the medication. "This can be done either by simply asking or in some cases administrating the medication itself," says Dr. Scheftner.

- **Accept your limitations.** You can't make someone else's depression go away and you're not to blame for the disease. "I would get frustrated sometimes when Mark called me because I didn't know how to handle it and thought he should be talking to his doctor because I felt inadequate," says my sister Shawn.

- **Get screened yourself.** Depression often runs in families. For the Litzsingers, depression had its roots in my mother's family. Of my immediate family, initially my mother and I had depression. Later some of my siblings, nieces, and nephews showed signs of depression as well. "We were battling depression on a lot of fronts [in] the family," adds Shawn.

- **Have patience.** Depression can take years to recover from, even when the person is receiving treatment from doctors. "I listened to Mark as he talked over and over and over about the same thing," says Robin. "I basically kept my mouth shut and just listened."

- **Don't ignore suicide threats.** "No matter how sick or tired or annoyed you are with the person's depression, never, ever condone or encourage suicide," stresses Dr. Scheftner. "To turn a person's thoughts away from suicide, list the people whose lives would be ruined and miserable forever as a result of that action—and get them professional help as soon as possible."

• **Keep the person involved.** Even though it's sometimes hard for a person with depression to mingle with other people, family members should encourage and cajole him into coming to events and gatherings. "Since Mark lived alone, I would bring him dinner," says my sister Heidi. "We tried to include him in things that we did as a family, be it a soccer game or whatever."

With all the progress in modern medicine, there's still a bit of mystery as to how depression impacts a person's brain, including why someone will respond wonderfully to a certain drug while another will not. "It's a difficult disease to have and to watch someone you love go through because you never know how long it will last," says my mother, Dona Litzsinger. "But even in the midst of Mark's depression, we knew we had to pull together to help him through it."

Part IV
The Recovery

Chapter 19

Patients and Recovery from Depression

"Sadness is a super important thing not to be ashamed about but to include in our lives. One of the bigger problems with sadness or depression is there's so much shame around it. If you have it you're a failure. You are felt as being very unattractive."

—Mike Mills, American musician

DEPRESSION RECOVERY ISN'T EASY—IN FACT, IT WILL BE ONE OF the hardest things you've ever done. Why? Because unlike an injury, there's no standard protocol with a reliable expectation as to the end result. In other words, with a broken arm, the doctor would set it, tell you how many weeks you'll need a cast, prescribe a certain amount of physical therapy in some cases, and then pronounce you healed. With depression, every person's experience and treatment will be different. Some recover in weeks, while some may take months or years. "In about 20 percent to 30 percent of people who have an episode of depression, the symptoms don't entirely go away."[342] That means, you might not feel normal for a long time or even remember what normal should feel like.

Around 19 million Americans currently live with depression, according to the National Institute of Mental Health.[343] That

165

association also pointed out that more than 80 percent of depressed patients who receive treatment say the treatment helps.

Not getting treatment or not completing the regime of treatment your doctor has prescribed can increase your chances of a relapse. Statistics from the American Psychiatric Association in Arlington, Virginia, show that at least half of those who experience a major depressive episode will have a second one. Also, around 80 percent of those having two episodes will have a third one.[344]

Those percentages shouldn't frighten you! Depression doesn't have to hang over your life. You have valuable information at your fingertips with this book, your doctors, family, friends, and your own experience with depression. Use it to help yourself during recovery and any future relapses.

Don't settle for feeling merely "okay." Instead, work with therapists and try medications and lifestyle adjustments to feel as good as you did before depression hit. We all have our ups and downs throughout our lives—it's what we learn from our challenges in life that make us stronger for the next hurdle we may encounter.

Understanding your issues clearly and charting the right course for a recovery strategy will be the roadmap to overcoming almost anything. With the tools, information, and education you get from professionals, you can create a route that is clear, organized, optimized, and focused. Be strong and ask those around you to be strong and supportive for you. Educate them like you have been educated and let them into your world to help. You would do the same for them.

Finally, don't give up—persevere! There is light at the end of the tunnel if you follow the medication and treatment protocol outlined by your therapist and doctors. Take it from someone who has lived the ups and downs of depression: Life is meant to be lived to the fullest. Everyone with depression can have a very normal life today. I lost years of my adult life because of this illness, and now my job is to use this book to get you to resources that can help resolve your issues with depression quicker, faster, and better. Some things in life are worth fighting for, and we are fighting together to get your life back on track.

The Stages of Recovery

How a person recovers from depression is highly personal, but there are some common emotional experiences[345] many people go through when battling depression. The stages of recovery are similar to the stages of grief and can include:

1. **Shock.** Many times those with depression are alarmed or surprised that they have the disease, especially when they have nothing upon which to base their understanding of what's to come.
2. **Denial.** Depressed people might have a hard time accepting this is the new "normal" for a while, especially because of continued stigma in the media and culture, as well as a lack of understanding as to effective treatments.
3. **Despair.** This emotion often is a symptom of the disease as well as a reaction to the diagnosis.
4. **Anger.** A close cousin of despair, a person might feel very angry at finding out he or she suffers from depression.
5. **Acceptance.** Finally, the person comes to the place of acknowledging that this condition has its challenges but also that there's hope of a better tomorrow.
6. **Coping.** Now the person finds new ways to live, new methods of tackling the symptoms, and new habits to instill to overcome depression.

At whatever stage you are currently, remember that support is available to help you on the road to recovery. From health professionals to family and friends, there are many along the way to lend you a helping hand as you work toward a bright future free from depression.

Chapter 20

Families and Recovery from Depression

"If you don't think your anxiety, depression, sadness, and stress impact your physical health, think again. All of these emotions trigger chemical reactions in your body, which can lead to inflammation and a weakened immune system. Learn how to cope, sweet friend. There will always be dark days."
—Kris Carr, American documentarian of *Crazy, Sexy Cancer*

DEPRESSION ISN'T A DISEASE FROM WHICH A PATIENT RECOVERS quickly. Many times the journey back to health is long and treacherous with setbacks along the way. This can be particularly difficult when you're watching a loved one make this trip. "My compassion for my brother grew, and I wanted to be there for him in any way I could because I couldn't comprehend what that would be like to live with depression every day," says my sister Robin. "But now that he's better, it's been a pleasure to see how fun and happy he is. He's engaging with his friends; he's a wonderful sibling. You want your siblings happy, so it's a relief to know he's okay."

"When Mark finally came out of the depression, it was like my brother was back," says my brother, Todd. "When he was on the meds and battling depression, he just wasn't as present. Now it's like you just found this person that you'd lost."

My sister Heidi adds, "His experience with depression helped me with my own situational depression. It's definitely in our family. My daughter has depression. Shawn and Todd have depression. We're all on medication and doing okay, but Mark was the one who helped me find my own balance. He recommended that I talk to my doctor about depression and that made all the difference."

As my own experience shows, family and friends are vital to a person's recovery from depression. It's so important to have their support and acceptance with a mental disease like depression because when you're in the midst of a depressive episode, your own thinking becomes off-kilter. Once you're on the road to recovery, family and friends continue to have an important role.

Here are some things family and friends can do that will assist the depressed person in his or her recovery:

- **Believe the person will get better.** Knowing that my family believed I would overcome this disease was fundamental to my own recovery.
- **Instill hope by telling the person he or she can do the hard work necessary to get better.** During recovery, family members have to walk a fine line between encouragement and criticism. "Be compassionate about what they are going through because it's a medical process and there are a lot of things they can't participate in while working on getting a good chemical balance with medications," says my sister Shawn.
- **Assist the person in rebuilding his or her self-image by helping to parse out the depression symptoms from the individual's real personality.** I now always recommend talk therapy with a professional as

well as treatment from a psychopharmacologist. The combination really works well and can relieve some of the pressure on members of the family or friends. The talk therapist can help you sort out your depression issues and issues with everyday life by being a good listener and sounding board for the patient. The psychopharmacologist will be focusing on key indicators of how well the medication protocol is working and at what speed for the patient. It's a very focused approach.

- **Adjust your communication styles when a patient is exhibiting depression symptoms.** Although the disease can be very frustrating for family and friends, remember that the patient "needs you to be in a safe, calming place," says Shawn. "If you can't find it in your heart to be kind and helpful, then it's best to be distant. Criticizing a person in depression is like hitting a weak dog. They take it very seriously when they are being criticized."

- **Try not to nag or push.** It's a fine line between encouragement and pressuring. Treatment takes time, and sensitivity and support are most important. Keep the person who is ill busy and distracted by suggesting movies, walks, and exercise of any kind. Exercise is great because it releases chemicals in the brain like endorphins that make the depressed feel better. (See Chapter 15 for more on the benefits of exercise.)

- **Remember that hopelessness, disinterest, anxiety, and anger are all depression symptoms.** My family was always supportive and included me in their outside activities. We went to the grocery store or walked in the park together. My family members patiently listened to me, even when I was ruminating and unable to break my thought process. My family was also very positive in supporting my efforts to get well. In the beginning, their care and support was instinctual because they didn't understand what I was going through. Over time, by my educating myself on the disease, they became educated on the best way to support me during my depressive episodes.

- **Keep up your support.** At every stage, your continued love and acceptance can be vital to the person's recovery.[346] My family continues to be very supportive of me in all my endeavors.

As the loved one moves further into recovery from depression, family and friends also can help the person regain his or her life by tempering any expectations to be more realistic and reachable. Sometimes the patient might want to do too much, so guiding him or her toward a slower schedule that still moves forward can be a huge help.

Offer support as they take on new things and have a new focus on life. I've found many new interests and hobbies over the last decade or so, including showing dogs and collecting antique cars. Since the recovery, I have had so many new interests, and my mind and life have been broadened so much. I became interested in helping entrepreneurs think through new ideas and business applications. I broadened my knowledge in different industries by being an advisory board member. I am very interested in politics and global affairs in this country and abroad. I am constantly sending new ideas to my family company leaders for our business.

For me, I found myself more interested in helping others more through situations in normal life. It's not about race, religion, or what color your skin is—it's about being a human being and doing the right thing for each other. All the people on this planet are trying to survive and have as much happiness in their lives as they can. We all have a role to play in making each other's lives better. Being respectful, a good listener, giving our time to a worthy cause, and being a good person are what we are all taught.

Remind depressed people of how far they've come when negative thinking creeps back in and encourage them to seek medical attention if it starts to become more than an isolated incident. Help them to look back on how far they've come and to enjoy where they are today.[347]

I've spent several years sharing my experience with patients, doctors, and family members in talks at Rush University Medical Center in Chicago, Illinois. After my last tough depression and recovery, I knew I was really lucky and feeling great. I approached my doctor, Dr. Scheftner, and told him that I wanted to give back and help those with depression. If they held public seminars on depression, I wanted to help in any way I could. I was not embarrassed by my depression and wanted to help and inspire patients and their families with my story, encouraging those in need to get help, stay focused, be determined, and never give up.

Since my initial meeting with Dr. Scheftner, Dr. Mark Pollack became the chairman of the Psychiatry Department at Rush University Medical Center. Dr. Scheftner introduced me to Dr. Pollack five years ago. Dr. Pollack and I talked about the idea of telling my story to others in conjunction with seminars he and his associates were doing for the public at different venues in the Chicago area. He liked the idea of a patient telling his story because it added an element of realism and connection. Since that time, I have spoken three times with Dr. Pollack and his wonderful staff. "In an odd, strange way, what Mark has gone through has helped a lot of people figure out what depression does," says Heidi.

I'm grateful that I've been able to use my depression to help others, whether it's patients who have the disease, family members, or medical professionals. I've been blessed with a full recovery, and now use my knowledge and understanding to impact a wider range of people. "Mark has taught me so much, a whole world about compassion and when to use and how to use it. We've all grown so much from this disease—in some ways it's our blessing," says Shawn. "Because every family gets hit with something, and those things that are hard are the things that really grow the family and bring the family together."

Conclusion

"A journey of a thousand miles must begin with a single step."
—Lao Tzu, Chinese philosopher

Oɴᴇ ᴏꜰ ᴛʜᴇ ɢᴏᴀʟꜱ ᴏꜰ ᴛʜɪꜱ ʙᴏᴏᴋ ɪꜱ ᴛᴏ ᴍᴀᴋᴇ ᴅᴇᴘʀᴇꜱꜱɪᴏɴ ꜱᴇᴇᴍ normal. That might sound strange if you have depression, but I want to normalize the disease in a way that people—those who have it, those with family members who have it, and the public at large—view it as a relatively "normal" disease, one that can be beaten like cancer.

Depression has a far wider reach than one would expect. "Depression will be the number two illness in the next year," says Dr. Pollack. Here are some statistics that show just how great an impact depression has on the world.

- 350 million: The number of people affected by some form of the disease[348]
- 16 million: Estimated number of U.S. adults with at least one major depression in 2012[349]
- 41,149: Number of suicide deaths related to depression in 2013[350]
- 80 billion dollars: Estimated yearly cost of depression in the United States due to health-care and lost productivity at work[351]
- 10 to 20 weeks: The average number of weeks for psychotherapy treatments for depression.[352]

This book has covered the many different areas of depression. It also tells the true story of my personal struggle—and that of my family—with depression. It is my hope that you will find this book a resource of important information for patients, families, doctors, friends, and therapists to help each other in the war against this disease.

For those suffering from depression, I hope my story will inspire you to persevere and never give up hope! In my case, my journey was a roller-coaster ride over many years. There are more modern drugs today than when I was first diagnosed nearly four decades ago. These newer medications have far fewer side effects and are more effective in their end results. The search continues to find better and faster ways of treating this illness. However, the brain is the last frontier in medicine about which we still have a lot to learn.

Finally, without a doubt there can be a "light at the end of the tunnel" for all who have depression. Proper diagnosis; the right psychopharmacologist, talk therapist, and other health-care assistance; and focus, patience, and a never-give-up attitude by patients, family/friends, and doctors are the winning strategy.

Resources

"Every man has his secret sorrows which the world knows not; and often times we call a man cold when he is only sad."
—Henry Wadsworth Longfellow, American poet

T HE FOLLOWING ARE SOME OF THE MANY RESOURCES AVAILABLE TO those suffering from depression or for families and friends of depressed patients. All phone numbers and websites were accurate at the time of publication.

GENERAL INFORMATION ON DEPRESSION

Anxiety and Depression Association of America
Silver Spring, Maryland
240-485-1001
www.adaa.org
Offers resources and information on depression.

Beyondblue.org
www.beyondblue.org.au/
An Australian site that offers resources and information about depression, including an online live-chat option.

Mental Health America
Alexandria, Virginia
703-684-7722
800-969-6642
www.mentalhealthamerica.net
Offers resources and information on depression.

National Association of Mental Illness
Arlington, Virginia
703-524-7600
800-950-6264 (helpline)
www.nami.org
Offers resources and information on depression, including a toll-free helpline.

National Institute of Mental Health
Bethesda, Maryland
1-866-615-6464 (toll-free)
www.nimh.nih.gov/site-info/contact-nimh.shtml
Offers resources and information on depression, including an online live-chat option.

Suicide Prevention Hotlines
800-SUICIDE (800-784-2433)
800-273-TALK (800-273-8255)
800-799-4889 (for the hearing impaired)

ANIMAL THERAPY

Alliance of Therapy Dogs
877-843-7364
www.therapydogs.com

Provides support to members involved in animal-assisted activities.

American Kennel Club
www.akc.org/events/title-recognition-program/therapy/organizations/
Offers a list of therapy dog organizations across the
United States.

Pet Partners
Bellevue, Washington
425-679-5500
Petpartners.org
Provides animal-assisted therapy, activities, and education.

Saratoga WarHorse
Saratoga Springs, New York 12866
518-886-8131
www.saratogawarhorse.com
Offers veterans a three-day experience that has proven to be effective and invaluable for those struggling to adjust to life after military service.

NUTRITIONISTS

Academy of Nutrition and Dietetics
www.eatright.org
Has a find-an-expert search option for registered dietitian nutritionists on its website.

American Nutrition Association
Americannutritionassociation.org
Offers a find-a-practitioner search on its website.

National Association of Nutrition Professionals
www.nanp.org
Provides a list of board-certified holistic nutrition members.

PERSONAL TRAINERS

Association of Personal Trainers
www.associationofpersonaltrainers.org
Offers a find-a-trainer option on its website.

THERAPISTS

Good Therapy
888-563-2112, ext. 1
www.goodtherapy.org
Offers a nationwide directory of therapists.

FURTHER READING SUGGESTIONS

Research into depression continues to generate new ideas and studies. Here are some articles and books for further reading on the subject.

"Brain Training for Anxiety, Depression and Other Mental Conditions" by Andrea Petersen. *The Wall Street Journal.* 18 January 2016. http://www.wsj.com/articles/brain-training-for-anxiety-depression-and-other-mental-conditions-1453144315. Accessed 1/27/16.

"Chicago's Mental Health 'Crisis': Is Reform of Police Enough?" *Christian Science Monitor.* 29 January 2016. http://www.csmonitor.com/USA/Justice/2016/0129/Chicago-s-mental-health-crisis-Is-reform-of-police-enough. Accessed 2/3/16.

Darkness Visible: A Memoir of Madness by William Styron. From the Amazon.com description: "A work of great personal courage and a literary tour de force, this bestseller is Styron's true account of his descent into a crippling and almost suicidal depression. Styron is perhaps the first writer to convey the full terror of depression's psychic landscape, as well as the illuminating path to recovery."

"Hayden Panettiere Returns to Work Following Battle with Postpartum Depression." Yahoo News. https://www.yahoo.com/news/hayden-panettiere-returns-to-work-following-battle-134443339.html

"Hot Wired for Happiness?" by Amy Ellis Nutt. *The Washington Post*. 4 March 2016. http://www.washingtonpost.com/sf/national/2016/03/03/brain-hacking-hot-wired-for-happiness/

Man's Search for Meaning by Viktor E. Frankl. From the Amazon.com description: "Psychiatrist Viktor Frankl's memoir has riveted generations of readers with its descriptions of life in Nazi death camps and its lessons for spiritual survival."

"Panel Calls for Depression Screenings During and After Pregnancy" by Pam Belluck. *New York Times*. 26 January 2016. http://mobile.nytimes.com/2016/01/27/health/post-partum-depression-test-epds-screening-guidelines.html?smprod=nytcore-iphone&smid=nytcore-iphone-share&referer=&_r=0. Accessed 1/27/16.

Posttraumatic Stress Syndrome information. http://www.ptsd.va.gov/public/PTSD-overview/basics/how-common-is-ptsd.asp. Accessed 2/3/16.

"Solutions for Stressed-Out High-School Students" by Nikhil Goyal. *The Wall Street Journal*. 12 February 2016. http://www.wsj.com/articles/solutions-for-stressed-out-high-school-students-1455301683. Accessed 2/16/16.

"Villanova's Game-Winner: Why We Watch Sports" by Jason Gay. *The Wall Street Journal*. 5 April 2016. http://www.wsj.com/articles/villanovas-game-winner-why-we-watch-sports-1459870607. Accessed 4/6/16.

"'You're Not Alone!' We're Starting a Conversation about Anxiety, Depression, Help and Hope." *Oprah Magazine*. February 2016. http://www.oprah.com/.

INSPIRATIONAL VIEWINGS

I put these under the "never give up" and encouraging category.

"Bretagne—Dog's Best Day." https://www.youtube.com/embed/ezcHy8DkrmE?rel=0. Accessed 2/16/16.

"God Bless the USA" performance by the Texas Tenors. https://www.youtube.com/embed/daqwGRdRIsk?feature=player_detailpage. Accessed 2/16/16.

"So God Made a Dog." http://videos2view.net/God-made-a-dog.htm. Accessed 2/24/16.

"TCU Erases 31-point Deficit to Beat Oregon in 3OT in Valero Alamo Bowl." 3 January 2016. http://espn.go.com/college-football/recap?gameId=400852741. Accessed 2/16/16.

Bibliography

"There are far, far better things ahead than anything we leave behind."

—C. S. Lewis, British writer

ARTICLES

Abate, Carolyn. "The Best Depression Apps of the Year." Medically reviewed by Timothy J. Legg, PhD, CRNP. Healthline.com. 18 May 2017. http://www.healthline.com/health/depression/top-iphone-android-apps#2. Accessed 9/10/17.

"Antidepressants for Children and Teens." Mayo Clinic Staff. MayoClinic.org. http://www.mayoclinic.org/diseases-conditions/teen-depression/in-depth/antidepressants/ART-20047502. Accessed 9/1/17.

Asa, Richard. "Dangers of Helicopter Parenting When Your Kids Are Teens." ChicagoTribune.com. 23 June 2015. http://www.chicagotribune.com/lifestyles/sc-fam-0630-teen-helicopter-parent-20150623-story.html. Accessed 9/20/17.

Bakker, David, Nikolaos Kazantzis, Debra Rickwood, and Nikki Rickard. "Mental Health Smartphone Apps: Review and Evidence-Based Recommendations for Future Developments." *JMIR Mental Health*. 2016 Jan–Mar. 3(1): e7. Published online 1 March 2016. https://www.ncbi.nlm.nih.gov/pmc/articles/PMC4795320/. Accessed 9/11/17.

Bergland, Christopher. "Parental Warmth Is Crucial for a Child's Well-Being: Toxic Childhood Stress Alters Neural

Responses Linked to Illness in Adulthood." Psychology Today.com. 4 October 2013. https://www.psychologytoday.com/blog/the-athletes-way/201310/parental-warmth-is-crucial-child-s-well-being. Accessed 9/21/17.

Bobinchock, Adriana. "New Treatment for Depression Shows Immediate Results." *Harvard Gazette*. 28 July 2014. http://news.harvard.edu/gazette/story/2014/07/new-treatment-for-depression-shows-immediate-results/ Accessed 10/16/15.

Borresen, Kelsey. "Artist Channels How Depression Feels into Beautiful Drawings." Healthy Living section of *The Huffington Post*. 11 August 2017. http://www.huffingtonpost.com/entry/artist-depression-illustrations_us_598cd864e4b090964295eef3?ncid=APPLENEWS00001. Accessed 08/30/17.

Buhr, Sarah. "Huddle Is a Mental Health App That Aims to Be a Safe Space to Share with Peers." Techcrunch.com. 15 August 2017. https://techcrunch.com/2017/08/15/huddle-is-a-mental-health-app-that-aims-to-be-a-safe-space-to-share-with-peers/amp/. Accessed 9/2/17.

Cha, Ariana Eunjung. "More Than a Third of Teenage Girls Experience Depression, New Study Says." *The Washington Post*. 31 May 2017. https://www.washingtonpost.com/news/to-your-health/wp/2017/05/31/more-than-a-third-of-teenage-girls-experience-depression-new-study-says/?utm_term=.c4a7dd6223ca. Accessed 8/19/17.

DeRubeis, Robert J., Greg J. Siegle, and Steven D. Hollon. "Cognitive Therapy vs. Medications for Depression: Treatment Outcomes and Neural Mechanisms." *Nature Reviews Neuroscience*. Nature.com. October 2008. 788–796. http://www.nature.com/nrn/journal/v9/n10/full/nrn2345.html. Accessed 11/13/15.

"Depression in Children and Teens." *American Academy of Child & Adolescent Psychiatry*. No. 4; Updated July 2013.

http://www.aacap.org/AACAP/Families_and_Youth/Facts_
for_Families/FFF-Guide/The-Depressed-Child-004.aspx.
Accessed 9/1/17.

"Depression Facts." U.S. Centers for Disease Control and Prevention website.http://www.cdc.gov/nchs/fastats/depression.
htm. Accessed 12/3/15.

"Depression (Major Depressive Disorder)." MayoClinic.org.
22 July 2015. http://www.mayoclinic.org/diseases-condi
tions/depression/basics/definition/con-20032977. Accessed
9/12/15.

"Depression Recovery: An Overview." WebMD.com. 8 February 2014. http://www.webmd.com/depression/recovery-
overview. Accessed 12/3/15.

Diamond, Stephen A., Ph.D. "The Psychology of Psychopharmacology." PsychologyToday.com. 18 April 2008. https://
www.psychologytoday.com/blog/evil-deeds/200804/the-
psychology-psychopharmacology. Accessed 10/16/15.

Doheny, Kathleen. "Pets for Depression and Health: Can Your
Depression Problems Improve When You Interact with
Your Pet?" WebMD.com. 3 August 2012. http://www.web
md.com/depression/features/pets-depression. Accessed
11/13/15.

Dryden-Edwards, Roxanne, M.D. "Teen Depression." Medicine
Net.com. http://www.medicinenet.com/teen_depression/
article.htm. Accessed 8/26/17.

"Electroconvulsive Therapy (ECT)." MayoClinic.org. 25 October 2012. http://www.mayoclinic.org/tests-procedures/elec
troconvulsive-therapy/basics/definition/PRC-20014161.
Accessed 9/24/15.

"Family and Friends' Guide to Recovery from Depression and Bipolar Disorder." Depression and Bipolar Support Alliance.
2006. http://www.dbsalliance.org/pdfs/FamilyBookFinal.
pdf. Accessed 12/3/15.

Fink, M. "What Was Learned: Studies by the Consortium for Research in ECT (CORE) 1997–2011." U.S. National Library of Medicine National Institutes of Health. 12 February 2014. http://www.ncbi.nlm.nih.gov/pubmed/24571807. Accessed 9/24/15.

Fontana, Francesca. "Some Companies Want You to Take a Mental-Health Day." *The Wall Street Journal.* 17 August 2017. https://www.wsj.com/articles/why-some-companies-want-you-to-take-a-mental-health-day-1502789400. Accessed 08/30/17.

"Gene Therapy for Depression: A Futuristic Treatment." Mental HealthDaily.com. http://mentalhealthdaily.com/2015/08/21/gene-therapy-for-depression-a-futuristic-treatment/. Accessed 9/10/17.

"Google Has a New Feature Designed to Help People Suffering from Depression." CNN Money/Tech. 24 August 2017. http://money.cnn.com/2017/08/24/technology/google-depression-questionnaire/index.html. Accessed 08/30/17.

Greenlaw, Ellen. "Getting Started: Talk Therapy for Depression." WebMD.com. 6 July 2010. http://www.webmd.com/depression/features/therapy-therapist. Accessed 11/13/15.

Groberman, Alex. "Shock Treatments for Depression." PsyWeb.com. 23 May 2012. http://www.psyweb.com/articles/depression/shock-treatments-for-depression. Accessed 9/24/15.

Grohol, John M., Psy.D. "Alternative Treatments for Depression." PsychCentral.com. https://psychcentral.com/lib/alternative-treatments-for-depression/. Accessed 9/15/17.

Hall-Flavin, Daniel K. "Natural Remedies for Depression: Are They Effective?" MayoClinic.org. http://www.mayoclinic.org/diseases-conditions/depression/expert-answers/natural-remedies-for-depression/faq-20058026. Accessed 9/15/17.

Hendriksen, Ellen, Ph.D. "Is Your Gut Making You Depressed or Anxious?" QuickandDirtyTips.com, 23 December 2016.

http://www.quickanddirtytips.com/health-fitness/
mental-health/is-your-gut-making-you-depressed-or-
anxious?utm_source=sciam&utm_campaign=sciam.
Accessed 9/26/17.

Holmes, Lindsay. "11 Statistics That Will Change the Way You
Think about Depression." *The Huffington Post*. 21 January
2015. http://www.huffingtonpost.com/2015/01/20/depres
sion-statistics_n_6480412.html. Accessed 12/3/15.

Hurley, Dan. "The Return of Electroshock Therapy." *The
Atlantic*. December 2015. http://www.theatlantic.com/
magazine/archive/2015/12/the-return-of-electroshock-
therapy/413179/. Accessed 11/24/15.

Itkowitz, Colby. "Finding Hope on a Park Bench." *The Washington Post*. 18 July 2017. E1.

Jansson, Asa. "Mood Disorders and the Brain: Depression, Melancholia, and the Historiography of Psychiatry." Cambridge
University Press and U.S. National Library of Medicine,
National Institutes of Health. July 2011. http://www.ncbi.
nlm.nih.gov/pmc/articles/PMC3143872/. Accessed 9/4/15.

Kelly, Kate. "How Loneliness Can Impact Kids with Learning and Attention Issues." Understood.org. https://
www.understood.org/en/friends-feelings/managing-
feelings/loneliness-sadness-isolation/how-loneliness-
can-impact-kids-with-learning-and-attention-issues.
Accessed 9/20/17.

"Ketamine: The Future of Depression Treatment?" Web
MD.com. 23 September 2014. http://www.webmd.com/
depression/news/20140923/ketamine-depression#1. Accessed 9/1/17.

Kirsch, Irving, M.D. "Antidepressants and the Placebo Effect." *Zeitschrift fur Psychologie* (*Journal of Psychology*),
Hogrefe Publishing, 2014. Volume 222, Issue 3. 128–134.

http://econtent.hogrefe.com/doi/abs/10.1027/2151-2604/a000176. Accessed 11/13/15.

Kluger, Jeffrey. "New Clues to Depression Spotted in the Genome."Time.com. 1 August 2016. http://time.com/4431292/depression-genome/. Accessed 9/9/17.

Knapton, Sarah. "Depression Is a Physical Illness Which Could Be Treated with Anti-inflammatory Drugs, Scientists Suggest." *The Telegraph*. 8 September 2017. http://www.telegraph.co.uk/science/2017/09/08/depression-physical-illness-could-treated-anti-inflammatory. Accessed 9/12/17.

"Lack of Parental Support during Childhood Is Associated with Increased Adult Depression and Chronic Health Problems, Study Finds." American Psychological Association. 21 March 2004. http://www.apa.org/news/press/releases/2004/03/parental-support.aspx. Accessed 9/20/17.

Landau, Elizabeth. "Dogs First Domesticated in Europe, Study Says." CNN. 14 November 2013. http://www.cnn.com/2013/11/14/health/dogs-domesticated-europe. Accessed 11/24/15.

Lalayants, Marina, and Jonathan D. Prince. "Loneliness and Depression or Depression-Related Factors among Child Welfare-Involved Adolescent Females." *Child and Adolescent Social Work Journal*. April 2015, Volume 32, Issue 2, 167–176. https://link.springer.com/article/10.1007/s10560-014-0344-6. Accessed 9/21/17.

Lien, Tracey. "Depressed But Can't See a Therapist? This Chatbot Could Help." *Los Angeles Times*. 23 August 2017. http://www.latimes.com/business/technology/la-fi-tn-woebot-20170823-htmlstory.html. Accessed 9/10/17.

Ludwig, Sarah E. "Helping Young Adult Children Cope with Depression." MentalHealthTreatment.net. http://mentalhealthtreatment.net/helping-young-adult-children-cope-with-depression. Accessed 8/25/17.

Lythcott-Haims, Judith. "Kids of Helicopter Parents Are Sputtering Out." *How to Raise an Adult: Break Free of the Overparenting Trap and Prepare Your Kid for Success*, excerpt on Slate.com. 5 July 2015. http://www.slate.com/articles/double_x/doublex/2015/07/helicopter_parenting_is_increasingly_correlated_with_college_age_depression.html. Accessed 9/20/17.

"Major Depression among Adolescents." National Institute of Mental Health Staff. National Institute of Mental Health, National Institutes of Health. https://www.nimh.nih.gov/health/statistics/prevalence/major-depression-among-adolescents.shtml. Accessed 8/19/17.

"Mental Health Providers: Credentials, Services Offered and What to Expect." MayoClinic.org. 18 February 2014. http://www.mayoclinic.org/diseases-conditions/mental-illness/in-depth/mental-health-providers/art-20045530. Accessed 10/16/15.

Mitchell, Heidi. "To Treat Depression, Start with a Digital Therapist." *The Wall Street Journal*. 26 June 2017. R13.

Morris, Nathaniel. "Should People without Depression Take Medication to Prevent It?" *The Washington Post*. 17 September 2017. https://www.washingtonpost.com/national/health-science/should-people-without-depression-take-medication-to-prevent-it/2017/09/15/92623856-619b-11e7-a4f7-af34fc1d9d39_story.html?utm_term=.046f6f8aa244. Accessed 9/19/17.

Morris, Nathaniel. "Take a Pill to Ward Off Depression?" *The Washington Post*. 19 September 2017. E1, E5.

Nauret, Rick, Ph.D. "Long-Term Use of Opioids Ups Risk for Depression." PsychCentral.com. 13 January 2016. https://psychcentral.com/news/2016/01/13/long-term-use-of-opioids-up-risk-for-depression/97577.html. Accessed 9/2/17.

Nemade, Rashmi, Ph.D., Natalie Staats Reiss, Ph.D., and Mark Dombeck, Ph.D. "Historical Understandings of Depression." MentalHelp.net. September 2007. http://www.mentalhelp.net/articles/historical-understandings-of-depression. Accessed 9/4/15.

"New Depression Treatments Reported." ScienceDaily.com. February 2014. http://www.sciencedaily.com/releases/2014/02/140214130719.htm. Accessed 9/12/15.

Nierenberg, Cari. "7 Ways to Recognize Depression in 20-Somethings." LiveScience.com. 27 October 2016. https://www.livescience.com/56602-signs-depression-young-adults.html. Accessed 8/25/17.

Oaklander, Mandy. "The Anti Antidepressant." *Time*. 7 August 2017. 38–45.

Phillips, Michael. "Army Tests Injection for PTSD." *The Wall Street Journal*. 12 June 2017. 1. https://www.wsj.com/articles/can-a-single-injection-conquer-ptsd-the-army-wants-to-find-out-1497279572?mg=prod/accounts-wsj. Accessed 2/9/17.

Rao, Murali, M.D., and Julie M. Alderson, D.O. "New Depression Treatments Reported." ScienceDaily.com. February 2014. http://www.sciencedaily.com/releases/2014/02/140214130719.htm. Accessed 9/12/15.

Rao, T. S. Sathyanarayana, M. R. Asha, B. N. Ramesh, and K. S. Jagannatha Rao. "Understanding Nutrition, Depression and Mental Illnesses." IndianJPsychiatry.com. April–June 2008. http://www.ncbi.nlm.nih.gov/pmc/articles/PMC2738337. Accessed 12/14/15.

"Recognize the Warning Signs of Suicide." WebMD.com http://www.webmd.com/depression/guide/depression-recognizing-signs-of-suicide#3. Accessed 11/17/15.

"Recovery and Staying Well." Beyondblue.org. https://www.beyondblue.org.au/get-support/recovery-and-staying-well. Accessed 12/3/15.

Rothkopf, Joanna. "Autopsy: Robin Williams Had Lewy Body Dementia." Salon.com. 13 November 2014. http://www.salon.com/2014/11/13/autopsy_robin_williams_had_lewy_body_dementia. Accessed 11/3/15.

Ruiz, Rebecca. "Finally, We're Talking about Mental Illness Like Adults." Mashable.com. 13 August 2014. http://mashable.com/2014/08/13/robin-williams-mental-health-stigma/#yg3qCXjFa8qW. Accessed 10/28/15.

Sanders, Laura. "Microbes Can Play Games with the Mind." ScienceNews.org. 23 March 2016. https://www.science news.org/article/microbes-can-play-games-mind. Accessed 9/26/17.

Scaccia, Annamarya. "Could Party Drug Ketamine Be a Treatment for Depression?" RollingStone.com. 21 June 2017. http://www.rollingstone.com/culture/features/ketamine-future-of-depression-treatment-w488998. Accessed 8/19/17.

Schiffrin, Holly H., Miriam Liss, Haley Miles-McLean, Katherine A. Geary, Mindy J. Erchull, and Taryn Tashner. "Helping or Hovering? The Effects of Helicopter Parenting on College Students' Well-Being." *Journal of Child and Family Studies.* April 2014, Volume 23, Issue 3, 548–557. https://link.springer.com/article/10.1007/s10826-013-9716-3. Accessed 9/21/17.

Schmidt, Charles. "Mental Health May Depend on Creatures in the Gut." *Scientific American.* 1 March 2015. https://www.scientificamerican.com/article/mental-health-may-de pend-on-creatures-in-the-gut/?print=true. Accessed 9/26/17.

Serani, Deborah, Psy.D. "Genetic Testing for Better Depression Treatment." *Psychology Today.* 1 July 2014. https://www.psychologytoday.com/blog/two-takes-depression/201407/genetic-testing-better-depression-treatment. Accessed 9/12/15.

"Service Animals and Assisted-Animal Therapy." *reSearch*, Volume 8, Issue 1. National Rehabilitation Information Center.

http://www.naric.com/?q=en/publications/volume-8-issue-
1-service-animals-and-assisted-animal-therapy. Accessed
11/24/15.

Shedler, Jonathan. "The Efficacy of Psychodynamic Psychotherapy." *American Psychologist*. February–March 2010. http://
www.apa.org/pubs/journals/releases/amp-65-2-98.pdf. Accessed 2/8/16.

Shields, Brooke. "War of Words." *New York Times*. 1 July 2005.
http://www.nytimes.com/2005/07/01/opinion/war-of-
words.html?_r=0. Accessed 10/28/15.

Serpell, James. "Animal Companions and Human Well-Being:
An Historical Exploration of the Value of Human-Animal
Relationships." *Handbook on Animal-Assisted Therapy: Theo-
retical Foundations and Guidelines for Practice*. Cambridge,
Massachusetts: Academic Press, 2000.

Solovitch, Sara. "Onetime Party Drug Hailed as Miracle for
Treating Severe Depression." *The Washington Post*. 1 February 2016. https://www.washingtonpost.com/national/
health-science/a-one-time-party-drug-is-helping-people-
with-deep-depression/2016/02/01/d3e73862-b490-11e5-
a76a-0b5145e8679a_story.html. Accessed 2/8/16.

Stratton, Andrew. "Personal Trainer—History of This Practice." EzineArticles.com. 30 April 2010. http://ezinearticles.
com/?Personal-Trainer—History-of-This-Practice&
id=4206058. Accessed 11/24/15.

"What Is Neurofeedback?" International Society for Neurofeedback & Research pamphlet. www.isnr.org.

"What Is Psychopharmacology." American Society of Clinical
Psychopharmacology. ASCPP.org. http://www.ascpp.org/
resources/information-for-patients/what-is-psychophar
macology. Accessed 10/16/15.

"Winston Churchill and His 'Black Dog' That Helped Win
World War II." National Alliance on Mental Illness. http://

www2.nami.org/Content/NavigationMenu/Not_Alone/ Winston_Churchill.htm. Accessed 10/30/15.

Young Adult Depression." Child Trends/DataBank Indicator. https://www.childtrends.org/indicators/young-adult-depression. Accessed 9/1/17.

Young, Joel, M.D. "The Effects of 'Helicopter Parenting': How You Might Be Increasing Your Child's Anxiety." Psychology Today.com. 25 January 2017. https://www.psychologyto day.com/blog/when-your-adult-child-breaks-your-heart/ 201701/the-effects-helicopter-parenting. Accessed 9/20/17.

BOOKS

Andrews, Linda Wasmer. *Encyclopedia of Depression*. Santa Barbara, California: Greenwood, 2010.

Arkham, J. C., Christopher J. Garcia, and Chuck Serface. *Claims Department: Robin Williams Memorial: Comedian, Actor, Legend*. Lernersville, North Carolina: Office Supply Publishing, 2014.

Burgess, Wes. *The Depression Answer Book: Professional Answers to More Than 275 Critical Questions about Medication, Therapy, Support & More*. Naperville, Illinois: Sourcebooks, Inc., 2009.

Clak, David A., and Aaron T. Beck, M.D. *Scientific Foundations of Cognitive Theory and Therapy of Depression*. Hoboken, New Jersey: John Wiley & Sons, Inc., 1999.

Dukakis, Kitty, and Larry Lye. *Shock: The Healing Power of Electroconvulsive Therapy*. London, England: Penguin Group (USA), Inc., 2006.

Emmons, Henry, M.D. *The Chemistry of Joy: A Three-Step Program for Overcoming Depression through Western Science and Eastern Wisdom*. New York, New York: Simon & Schuster, 2006.

Engel, Jonathan. *American Therapy: The Rise of Psychotherapy in the United States*. London, England: Gotham Books, 2008.

Ehrenberg, Alain. *The Weariness of the Self: Diagnosing the History of Depression in the Contemporary Age.* Montreal, Quebec: McGill Queens University Press, 2010.

Hirshbein, Laura D. *American Melancholy: Constructions of Depression in the Twentieth Century.* New Brunswick, New Jersey: Rutgers University Press, 2009.

Ilardi, Stephen S., Ph.D. *The Depression Cure: The 6-Step Program to Beat Depression without Drugs.* Cambridge, Massachusetts: Da Capo Press, 2009.

Irons, Chris. *Depression.* Basingstoke, England: Palgrave Macmillan, 2014.

Lawlor, Clark. *From Melancholia to Prozac: A History of Depression.* Bethesda, Maryland: Oxford University Press, 2012.

Marchand, William R., M.D. *Depression and Bipolar Disorder: Your Guide to Recovery.* Boulder, Colorado: Bull Publishing Company, 2012.

Phelps, Jim, M.D. *Why Am I Still Depressed?: Recognizing and Managing the Ups and Downs of Bipolar II and Soft Bipolar Disorder.* New York, New York: McGraw-Hill, 2006.

Sharpe, Katherine. *Coming of Age on Zoloft: How Antidepressants Cheered Us Up, Let Us Down, and Changed Who We Are.* New York, New York: Harper Perennial, 2012.

Walker, Carl. *Depression and Globalization: The Politics of Mental Health in the 21st Century.* Berlin, Germany: Springer Science & Business Media, 2007.

Wehrenberg, Margaret. *The 10 Best-Ever Depression Management Techniques: Understanding How Your Brain Makes You Depressed & What You Can Do to Change It.* New York, New York: W.W. Norton & Company, 2010.

Weintraub, Amy. *Yoga for Depression: A Compassionate Guide to Relieve Suffering through Yoga.* New York, New York: Broadway Books, 2004.

Wright, Jesse H., and Laura W. McCray. *Breaking Free from De-pression: Pathways to Wellness*. New York, New York: Guilford Publications, Inc., 2012.

Zetin, Mark, Cara T. Hoepner, and Jennifer Kurth. *Challenging Depression: The Go-To Guide for Clinicians and Patients*. New York, New York: W.W. Norton & Company, Inc., 2010.

INTERVIEWS

Baumann, Heidi. Phone interview by Sarah Hamaker. Tape re-cording. 14 July 2015.

Cozzolino, Callandre. Phone interview by Sarah Hamaker. Tape recording. 25 August 2015.

Lee, Crystal I. Phone interview by Sarah Hamaker. 11 Septem-ber 2017.

Litzsinger, Dick. Phone interview by Sarah Hamaker. Tape recording. 1 July 2015.

Litzsinger, Dona. Phone Interview by Sarah Hamaker. Tape recording. 9 December 2015.

Litzsinger, Robin. Phone interview by Sarah Hamaker. Tape recording. 9 July 2015.

Litzsinger, Todd. Phone interview by Sarah Hamaker. Tape recording. 17 July 2015.

Norman, Suzanne. Phone interview by Sarah Hamaker. 15 September 2017.

Pollack, Mark. Phone interview by Sarah Hamaker. Tape record-ing. 26 August 2015.

Reimer, Deborahanne. Phone interview by Sarah Hamaker. 11 September 2017.

Rivera, Zak. Phone interview by Sarah Hamaker. Tape recording. 28 August 2015.

Scheftner, William. Phone interview by Sarah Hamaker. Tape recording. 22 September 2015.

Senner, Bonnie. Phone interview by Sarah Hamaker. Tape recording. 5 August 2015.

Stratman, Shawn. Phone interview by Sarah Hamaker. Tape recording. 2 July 2015.

Zakeri, Lynn R. Phone interview by Sarah Hamaker. 8 September 2017.

Footnotes

1 Scheftner, William. Phone interview by Sarah Hamaker. Tape recording. 22 September 2015.
2 Lawlor, Clark. *From Melancholia to Prozac: A History of Depression*. Bethesda, Maryland: Oxford University Press, 2012. 2.
3 Jansson, Asa. "Mood Disorders and the Brain: Depression, Melancholia, and the Historiography of Psychiatry." Cambridge University Press and U.S. National Library of Medicine, National Institutes of Health, July 2011. http://www.ncbi.nlm.nih.gov/pmc/articles/PMC3143872/. Accessed 9/4/15. 2.
4 Lawlor, 5.
5 Ehrenberg, Alain. *The Weariness of the Self: Diagnosing the History of Depression in the Contemporary Age*. Montreal, Quebec: McGill Queens University Press, 2010. 7 (preface).
6 Ibid., 24–25 (preface).
7 Jansson, 1.
8 Neergaard, Lauran. "Task Force Urges Doctors to Screen All Adults for Depression." Associated Press/*Washington Post*. 26 January 2016. https://www.washingtonpost.com/national/health-science/task-force-urges-doctors-to-screen-all-adults-for-depression/2016/01/26/9fb49fba-c44b-11e5-b933-31c93021392a_story.html. Accessed 2/3/2016.
9 Walker, Carl. *Depression and Globalization: The Politics of Mental Health in the 21st Century*. Berlin, Germany: Springer Science & Business Media, 2007. 45.
10 Andrews, Linda Wasmer. *Encyclopedia of Depression*. Santa Barbara, California: Greenwood, 2010. 473.
11 Walker, 47.
12 Ibid.
13 Irons, Chris. *Depression*. Basingstoke, England: Palgrave Macmillan, 2014. 183.
14 Borresen, Kelsey. "Artist Channels How Depression Feels into Beautiful Drawings." Healthy Living section of *The Huffington Post*. 11 August 2017. http://www.huffingtonpost.com/entry/artist-depression-illustrations_us_

598cd864e4b090964295eef3?ncid=APPLENEWS00001.   Accessed 08/30/17. 1.

15 Andrews, 473.

16 Walker, 47–48.

17 Stratman, Shawn. Phone interview by Sarah Hamaker. Tape recording. 2 July 2015.

18 Andrews, 473.

19 Walker, 46.

20 Andrews, 473.

21 "Winston Churchill and His 'Black Dog' That Helped Win World War II." National Alliance on Mental Illness. http://www2.nami.org/Content/NavigationMenu/Not_Alone/Winston_Churchill.htm. Accessed 10/30/15. 1.

22 Ibid.

23 Litzsinger, Dick. Phone interview by Sarah Hamaker. Tape recording. 1 July 2015.

24 Shields, Brooke. "War of Words." *New York Times.* 1 July 2005. http://www.nytimes.com/2005/07/01/opinion/war-of-words.html?_r=0. Accessed 10/28/15. 1.

25 Ibid.

26 Fontana, Francesca. "Some Companies Want You to Take a Mental-Health Day." *The Wall Street Journal.* 17 August 2017. https://www.wsj.com/articles/why-some-companies-want-you-to-take-a-mental-health-day-1502789400. Accessed 08/30/17.

27 Shields.

28 Rothkopf, Joanna. "Autopsy: Robin Williams Had Lewy Body Dementia." Salon.com. 13 November 2014. http://www.salon.com/2014/11/13/autopsy_robin_williams_had_lewy_body_dementia/. Accessed 11/3/15.

29 Ruiz, Rebecca. "Finally, We're Talking about Mental Illness Like Adults." Mashable.com. 13 August 2014. http://mashable.com/2014/08/13/robin-williams-mental-health-stigma/#yg3qCXjFa8qW. Accessed 10/28/15. 1.

30 Arkham, J. C., Christopher J. Garcia, and Chuck Serface. *Claims Department: Robin Williams Memorial: Comedian, Actor, Legend.* Lernersville, North Carolina: Office Supply Publishing, 2014. 37.

31 Andrews, 473.

32 List compiled from http://www.wcvb.com/health/14414700 and https://en.wikipedia.org/wiki/List_of_people_with_major_depressive_disorder. Accessed 10/30/15.

33 Reimer, Deborahanne. Phone interview by Sarah Hamaker. 11 September 2017.

34 "Depression in Children and Teens." *American Academy of Child & Adolescent Psychiatry.* No. 4; Updated July 2013. http://www.aacap.org/AACAP/Families_and_Youth/Facts_for_Families/FFF-Guide/The-Depressed-Child-004.aspx. Accessed 9/1/17.

35 Dryden-Edwards, Roxanne, M.D. "Teen Depression." MedicineNet.com. http://www.medicinenet.com/teen_depression/article.htm.   Accessed 8/26/17.

36 Ibid.

37 Lee, Crystal I. Phone interview by Sarah Hamaker. 11 September 2017.

38 "Major Depression among Adolescents." National Institute of Mental Health Staff. National Institute of Mental Health, National Institutes of Health.   https://www.nimh.nih.gov/health/statistics/prevalence/major-depression-among-adolescents.shtml. Accessed 8/19/17.

39 Ibid.

40 Cha, Ariana Eunjung. "More Than a Third of Teenage Girls Experience Depression, New Study Says." *The Washington Post.* 31 May 2017. https://www.washingtonpost.com/news/to-your-health/wp/2017/05/31/more-than-a-third-of-teenage-girls-experience-depression-new-study-says/?utm_term=.c4a7dd6223ca. Accessed 8/19/17.

41 Zakeri, Lynn R. Phone interview by Sarah Hamaker. 8 September 2017.

42 Nierenberg, Cari. "7 Ways to Recognize Depression in 20-Somethings." LiveScience.com. 27 October 2016. https://www.livescience.com/56602-signs-depression-young-adults.html. Accessed 8/25/17.

43 "Young Adult Depression." Child Trends/DataBank Indicator. https://www.childtrends.org/indicators/young-adult-depression.   Accessed 9/1/17.

44 Ibid.

45 Ibid.

46 Nierenberg.

47 "Young Adult Depression."

48 Nauret, Rick, Ph.D. "Long-Term Use of Opioids Ups Risk for Depression." PsychCentral.com. 13 January 2016. https://psychcentral.com/news/2016/01/13/long-term-use-of-opioids-up-risk-for-depression/97577.html. Accessed 9/2/17.

49 Ibid.

50 Ibid.

51 Dryden-Edwards.

52 Kelly, Kate. "How Loneliness Can Impact Kids with Learning and Attention Issues." Understood.org. https://www.understood.org/en/friends-feelings/managing-feelings/loneliness-sadness-isolation/how-loneliness-can-impact-kids-with-learning-and-attention-issues. Accessed 9/20/17.

53 Lalayants, Marina, and Jonathan D. Prince. "Loneliness and Depression or Depression-Related Factors among Child Welfare-Involved Adolescent Females." *Child and Adolescent Social Work Journal.* April 2015, Volume 32, Issue 2, 167–176. https://link.springer.com/article/10.1007/s10560-014-0344-6. Accessed 9/21/17.

54 "Lack of Parental Support during Childhood Is Associated with Increased Adult Depression and Chronic Health Problems, Study Finds."

American Psychological Association. 21 March 2004. http://www.apa.org/news/press/releases/2004/03/parental-support.aspx. Accessed 9/20/17.

55 Lalayants.

56 Bergland, Christopher. "Parental Warmth Is Crucial for a Child's Well-Being: Toxic Childhood Stress Alters Neural Responses Linked to Illness in Adulthood." PsychologyToday.com. 4 October 2013. https://www.psychologytoday.com/blog/the-athletes-way/201310/parental-warmth-is-crucial-child-s-well-being. Accessed 9/21/17.

57 Ibid.

58 Young, Joel, M.D. "The Effects of 'Helicopter Parenting': How You Might Be Increasing Your Child's Anxiety." PsychologyToday.com. 25 January 2017. https://www.psychologytoday.com/blog/when-your-adult-child-breaks-your-heart/201701/the-effects-helicopter-parenting. Accessed 9/20/17.

59 Asa, Richard. "Dangers of Helicopter Parenting When Your Kids Are Teens." ChicagoTribune.com. 23 June 2015. http://www.chicagotribune.com/lifestyles/sc-fam-0630-teen-helicopter-parent-20150623-story.html. Accessed 9/20/17.

60 Schiffrin, Holly H., Miriam Liss, Haley Miles-McLean, Katherine A. Geary, Mindy J. Erchull, and Taryn Tashner "Helping or Hovering? The Effects of Helicopter Parenting on College Students' Well-Being." *Journal of Child and Family Studies*. April 2014, Volume 23, Issue 3, 548–557. https://link.springer.com/article/10.1007/s10826-013-9716-3. Accessed 9/21/17.

61 Ibid.

62 Lythcott-Haims, Judith. "Kids of Helicopter Parents Are Sputtering Out." *How to Raise an Adult: Break Free of the Overparenting Trap and Prepare Your Kid for Success*, excerpt on Slate.com. 5 July 2015. http://www.slate.com/articles/double_x/doublex/2015/07/helicopter_parenting_is_increasingly_correlated_with_college_age_depression.html. Accessed 9/20/17.

63 Asa.

64 Dryden-Edwards.

65 "Depression in Children and Teens."

66 Ludwig, Sarah E. "Helping Young Adult Children Cope with Depression." MentalHealthTreatment.net. http://mentalhealthtreatment.net/helping-young-adult-children-cope-with-depression. Accessed 8/25/17.

67 Dryden-Edwards.

68 "Depression in Children and Teens."

69 "Antidepressants for Children and Teens." Mayo Clinic Staff, MayoClinic.org. http://www.mayoclinic.org/diseases-conditions/teen-depression/in-depth/antidepressants/ART-20047502. Accessed 9/1/17.

70 Ibid.

71 Ibid.

72 Ibid.

73 Cha.

74 "Depression in Children and Teens."

75 Dryden-Edwards.

76 "Young Adult Depression."

77 "Depression in Children and Teens."

78 Dryden-Edwards.

79 "Google Has a New Feature Designed to Help People Suffering from Depression." CNN Money/Tech. 24 August 2017. http://money.cnn. com/2017/08/24/technology/google-depression-questionnaire/index.html. Accessed 08/30/17. 1.

80 Ibid.

81 Litzsinger, Dona. Phone Interview by Sarah Hamaker. Tape recording. 9 December 2015.

82 Litzsinger, Robin. Phone interview by Sarah Hamaker. Tape recording. 9 July 2015.

83 Baumann, Heidi. Phone interview by Sarah Hamaker. Tape recording. 14 July 2015.

84 Stratman, Shawn. Phone interview by Sarah Hamaker. Tape recording. 2 July 2015.

85 Litzsinger, Todd. Phone interview by Sarah Hamaker. Tape recording. 17 July 2015.

86 Pollack, Mark. Phone interview by Sarah Hamaker. Tape recording. 26 August 2015.

87 Burgess, Wes. *The Depression Answer Book*. Napierville, Illinois: Sourcebooks, Inc., 2009. 108.

88 Ibid., 109.

89 "Mental Health Providers: Credentials, Services Offered and What to Expect." MayoClinic.org. 18 February 2014. http://www.mayoclinic.org/ diseases-conditions/mental-illness/in-depth/mental-health-providers/ art-20045530. Accessed 10/16/15. 2.

90 "What Is Psychopharmacology." American Society of Clinical Psycho-pharmacology. ASCPP.org. http://www.ascpp.org/resources/information-for-patients/what-is-psychopharmacology/. Accessed 10/16/15. 1.

91 Diamond, Stephen A., Ph.D. "The Psychology of Psychopharmacology." PsychologyToday.com. 18 April 2008. https://www.psychologytoday.com/ blog/evil-deeds/200804/the-psychology-psychopharmacology. Accessed 10/16/15. 1.

92 "Burgess, 110.

93 "Mental Health Providers: Credentials, Services Offered and What to Expect." 1.

94 Burgess, 110.

95 Ibid., 134.

96 "Mental Health Providers: Credentials, Services Offered and What to Expect." 1.

97 Burgess, 133.
98 "Recognize the Warning Signs of Suicide." WebMD.com. http://www. webmd.com/depression/guide/depression-recognizing-signs-of-suicide#3. Accessed 11/17/15. 1.
99 Ibid.
100 Hirshbein, Laura D. *American Melancholy: Constructions of Depression in the Twentieth Century.* New Brunswick, New Jersey: Rutgers University Press, 2009. 3.
101 Ibid., 12.
102 *Merriam-Webster Online Medical Dictionary.* http://www.merriam-webster. com/medical/allopathy. Accessed 1/18/16.
103 Hirshbein, 12.
104 Engel, Jonathan. *American Therapy: The Rise of Pyschotherapy in the United States.* London, England: Gotham Books, 2008. 9.
105 Ibid., 9.
106 Ibid., 71.
107 Ibid., 53.
108 Nemade, Rashmi, Ph.D., Natalie Staats Reiss, Ph.D., and Mark Dombeck, Ph.D. "Historical Understandings of Depression." MentalHelp.net. September 2007. http://www.mentalhelp.net/articles/historical-under standings-of-depression/. Accessed 9/4/15. 2.
109 Ibid.
110 Sharpe, Katherine. *Coming of Age on Zoloft: How Antidepressants Cheered Us Up, Let Us Down, and Changed Who We Are.* New York, New York: Harper Perennial, 2012. 35
111 Engel, 76.
112 Sharpe, 38.
113 Ibid., 39.
114 Ibid.
115 Clak, David A., and Aaron T. Beck, MD. *Scientific Foundations of Cognitive Theory and Therapy of Depression.* Hoboken, New Jersey: John Wiley & Sons, Inc., 1999. 37.
116 Ibid., 39.
117 Ibid., 39.
118 Ibid., 39.
119 Sharpe, 43.
120 Ibid., 36.
121 Engel, 242–243.
122 Ibid.
123 Ibid., 244.
124 Ibid., 249.
125 Ibid., 250.
126 Ibid.
127 Sharpe, 45.

128 Ibid., 44.
129 Engel, 251.
130 Hirshbein, 75.
131 Clak, 2.
132 Zetin, Mark, Cara T. Hoepner, and Jennifer Kurth. *Challenging Depression: The Go-To Guide for Clinicians and Patients.* New York, New York: W.W. Norton & Company, Inc., 2010. 26.
133 Rao, Murali, M.D., and Julie M. Alderson, D.O. "New Depression Treatments Reported." ScienceDaily.com. February 2014. http://www.science daily.com/releases/2014/02/140214130719.htm. Accessed 9/12/15. 1.
134 Wright, Jesse H., and Laura W. McCray. *Breaking Free from Depression: Pathways to Wellness.* New York, New York: Guilford Publications, Inc., 2012. 56.
135 Ibid., 39.
136 "Depression (Major Depressive Disorder)." MayoClinic.org. 22 July 2015. http://www.mayoclinic.org/diseases-conditions/depression/basics/definition/con-20032977. Accessed 9/12/15. 8.
137 Zetin, 1.
138 Ibid.
139 Burgess, 25.
140 Serani, Deborah, Psy.D. "Genetic Testing for Better Depression Treatment." *Psychology Today.* 1 July 2014. https://www.psychologytoday.com/blog/two-takes-depression/201407/genetic-testing-better-depression-treatment. Accessed 9/12/15. 1.
141 Wright, 42–43.
142 Ibid.
143 Ibid.
144 Zetin, 50.
145 Burgess, 24.
146 "What Is Neurofeedback?" International Society for Neurofeedback & Research pamphlet. www.isnr.org.
147 "Depression (Major Depressive Disorder)," 8.
148 Zetin, 408.
149 Ibid., 410.
150 Zetin, 410.
151 "Depression (Major Depressive Disorder)," 8.
152 Zetin, 408, 418.
153 Ibid., 418.
154 Burgess, 104.
155 Zetin, 419.
156 Ibid., 420.
157 Burgess, 104–105.
158 "Depression (Major Depressive Disorder)," 8.
159 Burgess, 46.

160 Zetin, 236.
161 Phillips, Michael. "Army Tests Injection for PTSD." *The Wall Street Journal*. 12 June 2017. 1. https://www.wsj.com/articles/can-a-single-injection-conquer-ptsd-the-army-wants-to-find-out-1497279572?mg=prod/accounts-wsj. Accessed 2/9/17.
162 Ibid.
163 Kirsch, Irving, M.D. "Antidepressants and the Placebo Effect." *Zeitschrift fur Psychologie* (*Journal of Psychology*), Hogrefe Publishing, 2014. Volume 222, Issue 3. http://econtent.hogrefe.com/doi/abs/10.1027/2151-2604/a000176. Accessed 11/13/15. 134.
164 Ibid.
165 Ibid.
166 Zetin, 50.
167 Wright, 5.
168 Burgess, 124.
169 Ibid., 126.
170 Ibid., 127–128.
171 Burgess, 25.
172 "New Depression Treatments Reported." ScienceDaily.com. February 2014. http://www.sciencedaily.com/releases/2014/02/140214130719.htm. Accessed 9/12/15. 1.
173 Ibid., 1.
174 Mitchell, Heidi. "To Treat Depression, Start with a Digital Therapist." *The Wall Street Journal*. 26 June 2017. R13. 1.
175 Ibid.
176 Ibid.
177 "Depression (Major Depressive Disorder)," 10.
178 Oaklander, Mandy. "The Anti Antidepressant." *Time*. 7 August 2017. 40.
179 Oaklander, 41.
180 Bakker, David, Nikolaos Kazantzis, Debra Rickwood, and Nikki Rickard. "Mental Health Smartphone Apps: Review and Evidence-Based Recommendations for Future Developments" *JMIR Mental Health*. Volume 3, Issue 1, 2016 Jan–Mar, e7. Published online 1 March 2016. https://www.ncbi.nlm.nih.gov/pmc/articles/PMC4795320/. Accessed 9/11/17.
181 Lien, Tracey. "Depressed But Can't See a Therapist? This Chatbot Could Help." *Los Angeles Times*. 23 August 2017. http://www.latimes.com/business/technology/la-fi-tn-woebot-20170823-htmlstory.html. Accessed 9/10/17.
182 Ibid.
183 Bakker.
184 Lien.
185 Bakker.
186 Buhr, Sarah. "Huddle Is a Mental Health App That Aims to Be a Safe Space to Share with Peers." Techcrunch.com. 15 August 2017. https://

techcrunch.com/2017/08/15/huddle-is-a-mental-health-app-that-aims-to-be-a-safe-space-to-share-with-peers/amp/. Accessed 9/2/17.

187   Abate, Carolyn. "The Best Depression Apps of the Year." Medically reviewed by Timothy J. Legg, PhD, CRNP. Healthline.com. 18 May 2017. http://www.healthline.com/health/depression/top-iphone-android-apps#2. Accessed 9/10/17.

188   Ibid.

189   Solovitch, Sara. "Onetime Party Drug Hailed as Miracle for Treating Severe Depression." *The Washington Post*. 1 February 2016. https://www.washingtonpost.com/national/health-science/a-one-time-party-drug-is-helping-people-with-deep-depression/2016/02/01/d3e73862-b490-11e5-a76a-0b5145e8679a_story.html. Accessed 2/8/16. 1.

190   Ibid.

191   Oaklander, 43.

192   "Scaccia, Annamarya. "Could Party Drug Ketamine Be a Treatment for Depression?" RollingStone.com. 21 June 2017. http://www.rollingstone.com/culture/features/ketamine-future-of-depression-treatment-w488998. Accessed 8/19/17.

193   Ibid.

194   Oaklander. 44.

195   Scaccia.

196   "Ketamine: The Future of Depression Treatment?" WebMD.com. 23 September 2014. http://www.webmd.com/depression/news/20140923/ketamine-depression#1. Accessed 9/1/17.

197   "Ketamine: The Future of Depression Treatment?"

198   Scaccia.

199   Ibid.

200   "Gene Therapy for Depression: A Futuristic Treatment." MentalHealthDaily.com. http://mentalhealthdaily.com/2015/08/21/gene-therapy-for-depression-a-futuristic-treatment/. Accessed 9/10/17.

201   Kluger, Jeffrey. "New Clues to Depression Spotted in the Genome." Time.com. 1 August 2016. http://time.com/4431292/depression-genome/. Accessed 9/9/17.

202   Ibid.

203   Oaklander, 44.

204   "Gene Therapy for Depression: A Futuristic Treatment."

205   Morris, Nathaniel. "Take a Pill to Ward Off Depression?" *The Washington Post*. 19 September 2017. E5.

206   Ibid.

207   Ibid.

208   Ibid.

209   Ibid.

210   Ibid.

211   Ibid.

212 Ibid.

213 Ibid.

214 Ibid.

215 Schmidt, Charles. "Mental Health May Depend on Creatures in the Gut." *Scientific American.* 1 March 2015. https://www.scientificamerican.com/article/mental-health-may-depend-on-creatures-in-the-gut/?print=true. Accessed 9/26/17.

216 Sanders, Laura. "Microbes Can Play Games with the Mind." ScienceNews.org. 23 March 2016. https://www.sciencenews.org/article/microbes-can-play-games-mind. Accessed 9/26/17.

217 Ibid.

218 Schmidt.

219 Ibid.

220 Hendriksen, Ellen, Ph.D. "Is Your Gut Making You Depressed or Anxious?" QuickandDirtyTips.com. 23 December 2016. http://www.quickanddirtytips.com/health-fitness/mental-health/is-your-gut-making-you-depressed-or-anxious?utm_source=sciam&utm_campaign=sciam. Accessed 9/26/17.

221 Sanders.

222 Ibid.

223 Hall-Flavin, Daniel K. "Natural Remedies for Depression: Are They Effective?"MayoClinic.org.http://www.mayoclinic.org/diseases-conditions/depression/expert-answers/natural-remedies-for-depression/faq-20058026. Accessed 9/15/17.

224 Norman, Suzanne. Phone interview by Sarah Hamaker. 15 September 2017.

225 Ibid.

226 Ibid.

227 Grohol, John M., Psy.D. "Alternative Treatments for Depression." PsychCentral.com. https://psychcentral.com/lib/alternative-treatments-for-depression/. Accessed 9/15/17.

228 Ibid.

229 Hall-Flavin.

230 Ibid.

231 Ibid.

232 Hall-Flavin.

233 Ibid.

234 Ibid.

235 Hurley, Dan. "The Return of Electroshock Therapy." *The Atlantic.* December 2015. http://www.theatlantic.com/magazine/archive/2015/12/the-return-of-electroshock-therapy/413179/. Accessed 11/24/15. 1.

236 Dukakis, Kitty, and Larry Tye. *Shock: The Healing Power of Electroconvulsive Therapy.* London: Penguin Group (USA), Inc., 2006. 1.

237 Ibid. 10.

238 Burgess, 105.
239 "Electroconvulsive Therapy (ECT)." MayoClinic.org. 25 October 2012. http://www.mayoclinic.org/tests-procedures/electroconvulsive-therapy/basics/definition/PRC-20014161. Accessed 9/24/15. 2.
240 Burgess, 105.
241 Groberman, 1.
242 Engel, 71.
243 Groberman, 1.
244 "Electroconvulsive Therapy (ECT)." 1.
245 Engel, 240–241.
246 Fink, M. "What Was Learned: Studies by the Consortium for Research in ECT (CORE) 1997–2011." U.S. National Library of Medicine National Institutes of Health. 12 February 2014. http://www.ncbi.nlm.nih.gov/pubmed/24571807. Accessed 9/24/15.
247 "Electroconvulsive Therapy (ECT)." 1.
248 Ibid., 6.
249 Ibid., 5.
250 Ibid.
251 Dukakis, 4.
252 Burgess, 105.
253 "Electroconvulsive Therapy (ECT)." 6.
254 Dukakis, 5.
255 Ibid., 10.
256 Marchand, William R., M.D. *Depression and Bipolar Disorder: Your Guide to Recovery*. Boulder, Colorado: Bull Publishing Company, 2012. 202.
257 Senner, Bonnie. Phone interview by Sarah Hamaker. Tape recording. 5 August 2015.
258 Greenlaw, Ellen. "Getting Started: Talk Therapy for Depression." WebMD.com. 6 July 2010. http://www.webmd.com/depression/features/therapy-therapist. Accessed 11/13/15. 1.
259 Ibid., 2.
260 Phelps, Jim, M.D. *Why Am I Still Depressed?: Recognizing and Managing the Ups and Downs of Bipolar II and Soft Bipolar Disorder*. New York, New York: McGraw-Hill, 2006. 231.
261 Ibid., 229.
262 Marchand, 204.
263 Phelps, 229.
264 DeRubeis, Robert J., Greg J. Siegle, and Steven D. Hollon. "Cognitive Therapy vs. Medications for Depression: Treatment Outcomes and Neural Mechanisms." *Nature Reviews Neuroscience*. Nature.com. October 2008. 788–796. http://www.nature.com/nrn/journal/v9/n10/full/nrn2345.html. Accessed 11/13/15. 788.
265 Wehrenberg, Margaret. *The 10 Best-Ever Depression Management Techniques: Understanding How Your Brain Makes You Depressed & What You Can Do to Change It*. New York, New York: W.W. Norton & Company, 2010. 7.

266 Marchand, 204.

267 Ibid., 205.

268 Shedler, Jonathan. "The Efficacy of Psychodynamic Psychotherapy." *American Psychologist.* February–March 2010. http://www.apa.org/pubs/journals/releases/amp-65-2-98.pdf. Accessed 2/8/16.

269 Phelps, 231.

270 Marchand, 213.

271 Ilardi, Stephen S., Ph.D. *The Depression Cure: The 6-Step Program to Beat Depression without Drugs.* Cambridge, Massachusetts: Da Capo Press, 2009. 191.

272 Ibid., 188.

273 Ibid., 174.

274 Itkowitz, Colby. "Finding Hope on a Park Bench." *The Washington Post.* 18 July 2017. E1.

275 Ibid.

276 Marchand, 216.

277 Wehrenberg, 5–6.

278 Greenlaw, 3.

279 Serpell, James. "Animal Companions and Human Well-Being: An Historical Exploration of the Value of Human-Animal Relationships." *Handbook on Animal-Assisted Therapy: Theoretical Foundations and Guidelines for Practice.* Cambridge, Massachusetts: Academic Press, 2000. 3–17.

280 Cozzolino, Callandre. Phone interview by Sarah Hamaker. Tape recording. 25 August 2015.

281 Landau, Elizabeth. "Dogs First Domesticated in Europe, Study Says." CNN. 14 November 2013. http://www.cnn.com/2013/11/14/health/dogs-domesticated-europe. Accessed 11/24/15. 1.

282 "Service Animals and Assisted-Animal Therapy." *reSearch.* Volume 8, Issue 1. National Rehabilitation Information Center. http://www.naric.com/?q=en/publications/volume-8-issue-1-service-animals-and-assisted-animal-therapy. Accessed 11/24/15.

283 Ilardi, 186–187.

284 Marchand, 229.

285 Phelps, 228.

286 Doheny, Kathleen. "Pets for Depression and Health: Can Your Depression Problems Improve when You Interact with Your Pet?" WebMD.com 3 August 2012. http://www.webmd.com/depression/features/pets-depression. Accessed 11/13/15. 2.

287 Marchand, 218.

288 Rivera, Zak. Phone interview by Sarah Hamaker. Tape recording. 28 August 2015.

289 Ilardi, 132.

290 Ibid., 15.

291 Ibid., 117.

292 Wehrenberg, 130.

293 Ilardi, 120.
294 Marchand, 219.
295 Wehrenberg, 130.
296 Ilardi, 119.
297 Ilardi, 243.
298 Wehrenberg, 122; Ilardi, 131.
299 Wehrenberg, 131.
300 Ibid., 134.
301 Weintraub, Amy. *Yoga for Depression: A Compassionate Guide to Relieve Suffering through Yoga*. New York, New York: Broadway Books, 2004. 131.
302 Ibid., 9.
303 Ibid.
304 Ibid.
305 Ibid.
306 Ibid.
307 Ibid., 10.
308 Stratton, Andrew. "Personal Trainer—History of This Practice." EzineArticles.com. 30 April 2010. http://ezinearticles.com/?Personal-Trainer—History-of-This-Practice&id=4206058. Accessed 11/24/15.
309 Wright, 269.
310 Burgess, 150.
311 Rao, 1.
312 Ilardi, 67.
313 Ibid., 74.
314 Rao, 4.
315 Emmons, Henry, M.D. *The Chemistry of Joy: A Three-Step Program for Overcoming Depression through Western Science and Eastern Wisdom*. New York, New York: Simon & Schuster, 2006. 78–79.
316 *Ibid*, 77–78.
317 Rao, 1.
318 Burgess, 155.
319 Ibid.
320 Wright, 270.
321 Ibid.
322 Burgess, 155.
323 Wright, 270.
324 Burgess, 151.
325 Wright, 26.
326 Rao, 5.
327 Emmons, 73.
328 Rao, 5.
329 Emmons, 74.
330 Ibid., 76.
331 Ilardi, 6.

332 Burgess, 152.
333 Wright, 26.
334 Rao, 3.
335 Ibid.
336 Emmons, 77.
337 Rao, 6.
338 Wright, 270.
339 Emmons, 72.
340 Burgess, 150.
341 Emmons, 76.
342 "Depression Recovery: An Overview." WebMD.com. 8 February 2014. http://www.webmd.com/depression/recovery-overview. Accessed 12/3/15. 1.
343 Ibid.
344 Ibid.
345 "Recovery and Staying Well." Beyondblue.org. https://www.beyond blue.org.au/get-support/recovery-and-staying-well. Accessed 12/3/15.
346 "Family and Friends' Guide to Recovery from Depression and Bipolar Disorder." Depression and Bipolar Support Alliance. 2006. http://www.dbsalliance.org/pdfs/FamilyBookFinal.pdf. Accessed 12/3/15. 5.
347 Ibid., 7.
348 Holmes, Lindsay. "11 Statistics That Will Change the Way You Think About Depression." *The Huffington Post*. 21 January 2015. http://www.huffington post.com/2015/01/20/depression-statistics_n_6480412.html. Accessed 12/3/15. 1.
349 Ibid.
350 "Depression Facts." U.S. Centers for Disease Control and Prevention website. http://www.cdc.gov/nchs/fastats/depression.htm. Accessed 12/3/15. 1.
351 Holmes, 1.
352 Ibid.